The Lure of
a Land by the Sea

The Lure of
a Land by the Sea

Venice Vignettes

delores hanney

for
the venice historical society:
the keepers of the past
for the generations of the future

with special thanks to
jill prestup
vhs president & journal editor

and for
william carroll, my bodacious one,
whom you shall meet on these pages

It was not about dreaming
but about living dreams.
Adam Braver

contents

preface

Venice, California sits here, at the far left side of the continent, the spot just before one falls off the edge. It began its existence as the physical realization of one man's fantasy facsimile of Venice Italy plunked down on the sun soaked Southern California coast: all canals and gondolas, Corinthian colonnades and high-toned attractions.

The welcome mat was flung out on Independence Day 1905 but almost at once the construct went south in favor of the public's preference for pursuits of a flashier kind. Within a year, it had taken on a far less classy, amusement zone air, the beginning of an unending reinvention that continues right into today.

This book holds a wide-ranging collection of little histories as strung across the continuum of a Venice timeline. Most first appeared in the quarterly journal of the Venice Historical Society. Embedded within the essays about the people and lifeways that have composed the gestalt of this incomparable place, in direct ways and subtle, you will find here whispers of what Venice was like in other times: the huge pipe that ran beneath the pier, the lima bean fields, the store window displaying false eyeballs.

Founder, Abbot Kinney, wasn't the only dreamer in the Venice, California firmament. Dream chasing is, indeed, at the heart of practically all the chronicles presented here.

foreword

I remember a Venice of mythic wonders, enjoyed as never-ending opportunities for mischief, pleasures found nowhere else and random accomplishments of questionable value.

It all began in 1920 when the Mother became manager of Villa City where she hosted visitors and permanents with equal ease. For me it was Miss Furrow's private school on Dudley Court at Trolley Way, where huge Red Cars thundered past every few minutes to make sure none of us kids fell asleep. I walked to school, which was no problem except for the day my tummy was upset and I didn't make it home in time. An icky little boy!

Later schooling was in Westminster Elementary on Washington Boulevard. I did well until the classroom bully got in my hair and I pounded his face into a desk. Administration moved me to another class wherein I was promoted to blackboard cleaner.

So tell me, where in the world could one find a tiny train parked downtown? Just give the conductor a coin and be rattled home serenaded by a steam engine whistle announcing the crossing of streets.

Or wander to a beach and ocean so clean you could be yourself without a care. And when the huge saltwater plunge appealed, swim there with noisy friends to dive for coins tossed by spectators. Perhaps these were the same people standing on the beach one evening of 1923 to watch a re-creation of the Dempsey-Firpo prizefight, as directed by continual telegraph messages from the New York ringside site.

Even the outside world was cared for. Visitors could arrive from as far as 50 miles away in Red Car electric trains.

Then walk across the street to a wonderful roller coaster, or eye-ball a random collection of stores on Windward Avenue leading them to the Venice pier; clustered with even more coasters, side-shows and a dance hall. Then, at the end of the pier, find Billy Ball's two marvelous launches, powered by twelve-cylinder air-craft engines, ready to hurl themselves over ocean waves in a trip to be long remembered.

I was too little to enter the Ship Café but Noah's Ark was for me. A crazy place. The tilt of the room made it appear that wa-ter was running up hill, that you were off balance and in trouble touching enough wall to keep from falling down. The Fun House was of even greater madness with spinning barrels to walk though and wonderful slides just right for us little people. For me it was heaven on earth with only an occasional bit of hell when I'd so easily manage to do it all wrong.

This was a special world where adults could laugh and gig-gle without shame, enjoy things they'd never dreamed of, and sample from a never ending supply of foods and liquids; all just a streetcar ride from almost anywhere in Los Angeles and adjoining counties.

Then there was the St. Marks Hotel where Jimmy the wait-er had a dog named "Bum" who's single trick began with guests laying a $1 bill on the floor so Bum could roll over on it, then carry the money to Jimmy. And Jimmy was no dummy either. He married my mother, quit waitering and opened a hamburger stand next to the pool hall. When he and mother would disappear to "take a nap" I was in charge. Cooking 'burgers on a grill was easy and many a customer received the world's greatest for only ten cents.

A bit later they opened the DeLuxe Café next to the Venice National Bank and I found work selling newspapers in front of the People's Drug store across the street. That didn't last be-cause I was too noisy and the store manager had me fired. Or perhaps I should not have clipped all those "Free Pier Ride" cou-pons from the *Venice Vanguard* to enjoy everything on the pier at no expense.

Next up was selling Sunday papers from a coaster wagon by walking down the center of the street and shouting the morning away. One day a buddy told me the bowling alley needed a pin-setter. But that night my mother was visited by a policeman who suggested that working in a bowling alley was not really the best thing for me.

For this was a Venice like no other place in the world.

A Venice that lives on in its delightful history and the joyous siren songs of Delores Hanney who tells it best of all in *The Lure of a Land by the Sea*.

William Carroll

Chapter 1

the developer's dream

Abbot Kinney was a traveler, a businessman, a humanitarian, a co-inventor of the Southern California milieu, as it existed at the end of the 1800s and during the early decades of the twentieth century. But most of all, Abbot Kinney was a dreamer. Venice-of-America was his most vivid dream. Here he envisioned a fanciful seaside quarter of beauty and bliss, where residents might live gracefully upon the banks of romantic canals, where visitors might find lovely lodgings, where a broad range of attractions brought uplift and gladness. Abbot Kinney made it all come to life.

His exotic, retro-Renaissance community began with the toss of a coin. The upturning of "tails" allowed Kinney to choose the swampy portion of the tract – seemingly suited solely to water foul – rather than to have it fobbed off on him by his less imaginative partners in the Ocean Park development, from whom the coin toss produced a welcome disconnection.

Right down to its glorification of high culture, to its uniform architectural style, to the lavish nighttime illumination and to the canals and lagoon and the faux sailing vessel parked upon the pier, Venice was fashioned after the 1893 World's Columbian Fair in Chicago, with a full measure of its City Beautiful concepts firmly intact.

The "City Beautiful" thought form was a philosophy of Progressivism that promoted the beautification of cities as a means to a good life for its citizens, theoretically fostering in said citizens a sense of contentment and cohesiveness and belonging that would inspire civic loyalty and dignified behaviors. The construct resonated so amiably with Abbot Kinney's own worldview that he embraced it without modification for his new ersatz Italian town beside the Santa Monica Bay.

He had a résumé fit for triplets. Previous to developing Venice, Kinney had been a tobacco buyer, an entrepreneur, a citrus farmer, a commissioner on the needs of California's mission Indians. He was a founder of libraries, a land subdivider, an advisor on the building of roads in L.A., a major in the California National Guard. He had been a member of the U.S. Geological Survey Team for the mapping of the Sioux Reservation and the creation of Yosemite National Park, the chairman of the California Forestry Bureau responsible for propagating eucalyptus trees all over the state. He was connected with several of Southern California's Railway systems, the owner of two Los Angeles newspapers for a time and a writer on a heroically wide field of subjects.

Honed during these earlier incarnations were the capacious skills he would need for the realization of a dream of such audacity as Venice-of-America, which opened on Independence Day 1905. Over the years a plethora of problems would surface to challenge him: the pier would be washed out, the sandy beach would shrink, sewage would pollute the bay, the canals would turn putrid, politics would prove as putrescent as the water in the ocean and canals. And folks weren't much interested in high culture amusements.

Abbot Kinney not only had range, he was tenacious as a terrier and as unshakably committed to the success of his Venetian Kinneyland as he was idealistic. So, he simply brought on bunches of livelier pleasures in the form of the Midway Plaisance: those carny/amusement park thrills left over from the 1904 Saint Louis World's Fair via Portland's 1905 Louis and Clark Exposition.

The term "master planned community" was not even a blip on a lexicographer's brainwave when Kinney hauled Venice into fully formed fruition: all harmonious architecture, open spaces and laudable amenities enhanced by technologies of the most edgy sort. Atmospherically swanned-out in Mediterranean drag, the auditorium, the bathhouse, the hotels, the music and dance pavilions, established a better-place ambiance inviting surrender to a felicitous lifestyle.

In some ways, Venice foreshadowed by exactly half a century Disneyland's self-contained world. Part myth, part metaphor, part stage set, visionaries Abbot Kinney and Walt Disney both created ingenious environments that were – by design – at once elevating and entertaining, wherein principles were utopianized and values made as tangible as gooey chocolate fudge sundaes.

But Disneyland is a privately owned world, as subject to the direction of the suits in possession as the animated films that they also produce. While Venice, on the other hand, leaps and limps in an evolutionary process choreographed by the vagaries of the often eccentric humanity that comes to this public domain – for an afternoon, or a year or a lifetime.

Chapter 2

vitalizing the vision

In Abbot Kinney – a man of brains and range and passion – the engineering solution to a land development dilemma exploded into a dream: Venice-of-America, a boldly rearranged marshland with a lagoon, canals and a distinctly Italianate gestalt into which he would import gondolas and singing gondoliers and even Italian pigeons after which he would name a street – Paloma Avenue – by way of cementing a rosy authenticity quotient.

I imagine the beachy air seemed almost perfumed with the scent of aspiration about to be fulfilled after Kinney invited Norman Foote Marsh and C.H. Russell to be the vision vitalizers who would bring the quixotic dream into real life existence. Recommended by the prestigious landscape architectural firm founded by "City Beautiful" evangelist Frederick Law Olmstead, the architects had studied classical architecture, they were young and enthusiastic and swiftly captivated by Kinney's romantic concept of a Mediterraneanized casbah upon the California coast.

To Kinney's credit he hired these men he judged to be sublimely suited to the job and then he stood back, with no micromanaging.

Envisioned, more or less, as a decreased size World's Columbian Fair in Chicago, it was yet a huge commission calling for the atmosphere-establishing design of a complete new city: its business district and residential areas and its series of canals spanned by picturesque bridges that emanated from the large central lagoon. It also called for the design of the chief theme-supporting public buildings.

In only 12 months, Marsh and Russell came through with such nimble ease one would have thought they were building pointy little sand castles rather than rendering stunning plans

5

for a nouveau Renaissance colony slightly south of Santa Monica. But Marsh articulated a pretty clear grip of the awesomeness of his and Russell's accomplishment when he referred to Venice as, "a magic city (built for the generations) with its stately arcades, shimmering lagoon, floating pennants and glistening minarets."

Between them they designed the forms for the plush auditorium, the bathhouse, the amphitheatre, the Hotel Windward on Trolley Way, the Windward Avenue hotels colonnaded with classical Corinthian columns and into which was pumped hot saltwater for therapeutic baths, the entrance to the Midway Plaisance, the Cabrillo restaurant and hotel – more popularly known as the Ship Café – as well as numerous others.

Kinney encouraged prospective merchants, businessmen and homeowners to stick with the Venetian program when erecting their own private structures. And though some of his hoped for installations did not materialize, most notably the University of the Arts, Kinney was essentially pleased and wont to proclaim, with promotional zeal, "to see *Venice* is to live!"

Despite their youth, when they joined up with Kinney, the firm of Marsh and Russell was already making a name for itself for upscale residences, churches and their first Carnegie library. However, their association was dissolved in 1907 with Marsh remaining in SoCal while Russell trundled off to San Francisco, though still contributing to the Venice effort.

Meaning no denigration of Russell's work, the fact is that as both a contemporary man and a historic figure Norman Foote Marsh was the alpha architect of the pair. Born and educated in Illinois, upon obtaining his Bachelor of Science degree from the School of Architecture at the University of Illinois, Marsh worked for a while in his home state as an engineer before heeding the call to relocate to the Los Angeles milieu so incredibly rife with opportunities for talented practitioners of the architectural profession.

Venice was, of course, the defining project of his career. How could it not have been? He would also earn an enviable reputation as a master architect of schools and universities and would continue to design churches of distinction. A South Pasadenan himself, Marsh designed the Carnegie library for that community. One of his most important undertakings was the Columbia

Hospital in Los Angeles; a facility smarted up with every then-conceivable cutting edge feature.

Married with children, he was not known as a joiner, generally avoiding the membership in clubs and organizations that most men of his time and station embraced.

Of the Venice Norman Foote Marsh and C.H. Russell conceived little is left, most conspicuously the iconic Windward Avenue colonnades, newly restored though the buildings they're attached to – with their upper floors lopped off – are mere semblances of what they used to be.

But it's enough. Enough to keep alive the connection of the past to the present and on to future; enough to prompt us to remember the power of a dream.

Chapter 3

drama queen

Sarah Bernhardt's appearance in Venice, California was a fabulous fluke brought on by her cross-dressing roles that set the L.A. League of Decency folks bonkers and unalterably disinclined to have her perform in their imagined-genteel community during her 1906 Farewell America Tour.

Abbot Kinney could smell opportunity wafting in the air like the scent of patchouli, and when Los Angeles officially pulled in its welcome mat he was on it as swiftly as a kitten on a cricket, whisking Bernhardt off to Venice, there to avail herself of his snappy 3600-seat auditorium for her three scheduled L.A. performances. She was sixty-one years old and the world's greatest actress; just the classy cultural entertainment he had envisioned for his Renaissancey seaside community.

When the ritzy railroad car borrowed from the New York Vanderbilts – wherein she had been traveling and dwelling graciously throughout the term of her tour – was duly ensconced on the tracks upon the pier, Kinney took himself off to personally make arrangements for the fishing in which his honored guest expressed an interest; arrangements that consisted of hiring some boys to hook a series of cod on her line.

All went splendaciously. She reveled in the glory of sublime sherberty sunsets from her perch on the observation platform of the posh Pullman car. She caught and consumed the carefully planted fish. She was fawned over by a little delegation of French ex-patriots led by the famed flower painter, Paul DeLongpre. She was wined and dined at the elegant Ship Café. And she was gratified that despite the fact that most of the theatergoers understood not a single word of French, her turns in *La Sociere, La Dame Aux*

9

Camelias and *La Tosca*, elicited twenty curtain calls and raked in buckets of money.

Sarah Bernhardt was the child of a prosperous Parisian courtesan. It was, in fact, one of her mother's "sponsors" who paved the way for her training and apprenticeship in the theatre.

Slim as a slip of bamboo and crowned by an abundance of bushy hair the color of ripe apricots warm from the sun, she was a right dishy damsel with an awesome talent for acting that she wielded with the finesse of a fencing master. Brazenly original, tragedy was Bernhardt's natural métier, why even her very name became a synonym for drama. She had a voice which was like a celestial harp, an "orchidaceous air," as one critic so deliciously described her; and though as wispy as a consumptive she was nevertheless possessed of a high-voltage intensity that left audiences now limp and weak, now thrilled and delighted, even in leading male roles such as Hamlet.

Though nonchalantly tempestuous and insouciantly rude she aroused faithful devotion, which she repaid in kind. Within her haphazardly furnished Paris home – that included a coffin in her bedroom – she encircled herself with an ardent little salon of the inspired, the amusing, and the brilliant. Many were numbered amongst the slew of former lovers that stayed on as friends when their tenure as her intimate liaison had ended. They were artists and writers, thespians and socialites, even a one-day-to-be king, and a menagerie of critters representing a disconcerting range of domestication.

Almost from the beginning she embraced revolutionary technologies: photography, sound recording, silent movies. She also recognized the self-promotion value of her image on advertisements or packaging for such mundane commodities as curlers or soap.

Before sallying forth in 1880 to wow U.S. audiences for the first time, with her incandescence and her power, she would already be the darling of Paris, of London, of Brussels and Copenhagen. Her 1906 Farewell America Tour was neither the first nor the last U.S. "farewell tour" Sarah Bernhardt made, but it was the only time that she ever played Venice. She did, however, stay in Venice once again, at the King George Hotel – later called the Ocean View – while appearing in Los Angeles in 1913.

It is said that in the 1950s a young James Dean would come to that same hotel where Divine Sarah once stayed, to seek out her spirit for wisdom on his own unfolding path as an actor. Quietly he closed the door to the room she had occupied, and lay down on the bed to commune with the thespian legend.

Perhaps that's only a story – but isn't it a swell one?

Chapter 4

wizard

At about the same time as Abbot Kinney was assembling his Old World repli-city with elevating aspirations some 16 miles southwest of L.A., Arthur Reese – in the guise of a Southern Pacific Railway porter – arrived in Los Angeles and recognized it as a promising place for a bright, energetic young black man with an entrepreneurial zeal simply panting to be uncorked. His impulse and impetus would lead him to be the first black businessman in Venice, the first black resident in the "whites only" enclave, even its first black election board member. For like Kinney himself, Reese was a dreamer and a doer of relentless dedication; like Kinney himself, Reese had a nose for opportunity.

Given the high level of excitement Kinney's new Venice-of-America was generating – circa 1905 – and the diligent researching and reconnoitering Reese undertook on where and how to begin his future triumphs, it would have been unnatural for him not to have boarded an interurban electric car to check out Venice. And so he did; and it came to pass that, armed with the necessary supplies, Reese was soon offering shoeshines in Venice with such stellar success that he had to hire a crew, then bicycles to meet the geographical expansion. Seeing this was good, he decided to branch out.

His next endeavor was inaugurated with a classified ad proclaiming "carpets beaten, cleaned and aired; furniture upholstered and repaired, houses freed from dirt and grease." He called it the Gordon Day Work Company, swiftly added window washing, maintenance and janitorial service to its menu and installed the company in offices on Windward Avenue. With a quickness, his new business' mops and pails and feather dusters were causing clean all over the area – and for such impressive accounts as the Santa Monica schools and the Ocean Park City Hall – all to a harmonious chorus of customer satisfaction.

It was almost inevitable that Reese would show up on Abbot Kinney's radar. And there he was: not only on his radar but also in his employ, managing the janitorial division of Kinney's empire at the same time he was managing his own. Occasionally he supervised simultaneous services.

The next steps on his path to utter ubiquity were as provisioner of towels for the beach, the bathhouse, the saltwater plunge, then as the decorating wallah for all manner of events and venues. At any given moment, Reese might have been found furiously flinging bunting about a Venice dance hall, wiring up what would be a first-generation mirrored disco ball, creating grape-festooned sculptures for a festival. From there, float making was just a logical deployment of his prodigious talent. His design work was acknowledged with awards and accolades, among them a Tournament of Roses first prize.

Ever alert to the possibility of a new enterprise, Arthur Reese and his brother Edward submitted an offer to assume the operation of the Venice Boat & Canoe Company after its boathouses on the lagoon went up in flames in the spring of 1920. By then, yet-to-be-diagnosed lung cancer was sucking the life force from Abbot Kinney, who must have felt hugely relieved to have a confirmed Venice-lover with proven commercial skills and a history of Louisiana bayou skimming in a flat-bottomed pirogue to take over his boating business.

Fifteen years later Reese would again invoke his Louisiana roots when he introduced Mardi Gras to the Venice scene. The three-day carnival unleashed parades and processions, a treasure hunt for the kiddies, a beauty pageant, a ball. Reese produced scores of huge, strange papier-mâché heads – weighing up to forty pounds – by way of which many of the merrymakers disguised themselves. Revelers rushed in by the thousands, reinstating the town's reputation as the premier destination for a good time, reinvigorating its finances.

Arthur Reese was a latter day Venetian Renaissance man of sorts with ambitions and aptitudes and accomplishments that leaked out in every which direction. Known in the realm as the "Wizard of Venice" he was simply "grandfather" Sonya Reese Greenland.

She remembers how he would swoop her up to go to ice-skating or to the circus, expensive entertainments her parents could not afford. She remembers accompanying him as he went about his work, not as labor but as enjoyable company. She remembers him introducing her to the architect Paul Williams. Fondest of all, she remembers how at Christmastime he would pick up a load of Christmas trees, which he fireproofed and flocked and delivered to everyone in their large extended family.

Chapter 5

suffragists at the seashore

*To my knowledge, there is no just
objection to equal suffrage.*
Abbot Kinney

The opinionated developer of Venice, California matched action
to thought in producing a "Suffrage Day" program held in the
new 3600-seat auditorium – filling it twice – on August 1, 1905,
less than a month after the gala grand opening of Venice. The
day's formidable line up included Susan B. Anthony, Reverend
Anna Shaw and Caroline Severance. Between sessions, The SoCal
Women's Press Club stood the ladies to a gracious high tea at the
Ship Café.

Susan B. Anthony was an impassioned octogenarian with
steely moral fiber and the constitution of a battleship. She cut her
cause-championing teeth on abolitionist and temperance issues
and, as a roving advocate for suffrage equality, she gave 75 to 100
speeches every year.

Like her pioneering friend and longtime sidekick in women's
suffrage promotion, Caroline Severance was 85. An L.A. trans-
plant, she founded the Friday Morning Woman's Club in Los
Angeles to nourish broader scope and institute her philosophy
which asserted, "*Nothing* is impossible to organized womanhood."

The comparative freshman of the group, at age 58, Anna Shaw
was an ordained Methodist minister as well as a medical doctor.
"With caustic wit and brilliant repartee [Shaw] vanquished all the
unconvinced," according to the *Los Angeles Herald*.

Back in 1893, the California legislature had already *passed*
a bill granting voting rights to the women of the state. After

noodling his way to the wrongheaded notion that the concept was unconstitutional, his honor, the governor, vetoed it.

And so the effort lumbered along, until October 10, 1911. Two anxious days later the vote count was complete, culminating in explosions of pride and congratulations. The state referendum was approved by a 4,000-vote margin, an average of just one vote per precinct. Thus California became the sixth state in nation in which women could vote and some historians report it was Caroline Severance who was the first California woman to do so. It was a full nine years before women's voting rights would go national.

While it took voting men to ultimately lift women's suffrage from nice idea to reality, the foot soldiers of the operation were, needless to say, women. And here they were well-served by the tendency of women – at that time – to be joiners of numerous organizations simultaneously – from church groups to labor unions, from china painters to book discussion groups and post-card exchange clubs.

"Suffragette" is a term coined by a snarky newspaper reporter by way of belittling women's effort to obtain, for themselves, the right to vote. In an in-your-face shift, these self-same women embraced the label as their very own preferred sobriquet.

Cranked up with the idealistic conviction that if women had the vote it would change everything, the determined suffragettes were hardnosed, clever and inventive. They presented plays and pageants and parades. They utilized snappy graphics on seemingly ubiquitous posters, pamphlets, flyers and leaflets – throwing in some buttons, pennants, stamps and seed packets for good measure.

In a stroke of unmitigated genius they acquired a sexy, provocative, man-pleaser of a car that they named the "Blue Liner." In it they tooled around the state, attracting men like ants to a picnic, then – while they were captives of the automobile's allure – regaled them with the merits of equal suffrage.

There's a rumored photograph of Abbot Kinney standing beneath a banner with five stars, signifying the states where women could already vote, and the words "California Next."

Diligent detecting has so far failed to uncover said photo. More's the pity.

Circumstantial evidence of the picture's likely existence – and real proof of Kinney's continuing support for equal suffrage – was unearthed from the fog of elderly microfilms of the *Venice Daily Vanguard*.

A tiny piece from the August 3, 1911 issue of the paper reports that when turned away by Los Angeles, Kinney extended an invitation to hang a banner – answering the "California Next" description – on Windward Avenue in Venice. A much longer article, on August 7th, tells of a humongous, plaza-filling crowd rallying under this banner. Men were well represented at the gathering, many wearing the event's yellow badge. Representatives of a whole bunch of civic groups were there too.

Analyzing the occasion, the journalist voiced his opinion that, "Beyond a doubt the woman suffrage campaign received a most beneficial impetus from this meeting."

As the centennial anniversary of women's suffrage in California is celebrated, these days more women than men are casting ballots.

lions & tigers & bears, oh my!

Alpheus George Barnes Stonehouse had a special affinity with the four-footed ones of the earth. For some men this might have translated into a career as a goat farmer, contrarily he was set onto a gaudier path as the owner of the Al G. Barnes Circus & Wild Animal Zoo. The commencement of his career as a showman was decidedly downscale, consisting as it did of a pony, a phonograph and a picture machine but it grew to require 40 railroad cars to transport the hundreds of entertainers, trainers, workers and animals on their 35,000-mile seasonal circuit mostly through the western United States and Canada.

In 1911, with circuses the most popular type of public amusement, Abbot Kinney cooked up a deal with Al G. Barnes for his traveling tented circus to winter in Venice. In consequence, late that November it arrived in the form of a fabulous parade with Barnes in full impresario mode riding atop Tusko – a ten-foot tall, seven-ton Asian elephant with extravagant nine-foot tusks – behind him a long stream of the circus' flamboyant acts and attractions.

The populace went wild! They could hardly wait to fill the seats for the four electrifying performances that would follow over the next couple of days. Later on there would be three weeks of Venice shows.

The roster of amazement-makers left no attendee disappointed! But, aside from geeks and freaks, people were the supporting cast and people-focused acts were not what Barnes was really up to. *His* circus was about trained animals and boasted more than in all the other circuses combined; among them fierce bears and lions, boxing kangaroos and juggling seals, singing mules and musical pigeons. There were scores of galloping horses carrying multiple species of performing passenger (though not all at once), Wally the orangutan and his kith and kin, Lotus the hippo.

The most famed of the show's entertainments was Mabel Stark and her tigers. Mabel was tiny, just 100 pounds; typically tigers weigh in at 550 pounds or more and are not reputed to be the most mild mannered of felines. But there she would be, inside a ring, in the company of ten or twelve of them, with nothing but a buggy whip between her and unqualified disaster. Several times she was seriously mauled and sliced. Rajah was the most beloved of her tigers, with him she developed the first-ever tiger vs. tamer ersatz wrestling match to well and truly awe the circus audience.

During their snowbirding months in Venice, Mabel and Rajah would be seen together peacefully walking along the sandy beach. On blessedly rare occasions other of the circus' wild animals were also seen unconfined: those times when elephants or camels escaped to thunder about on the pier and the streets of their winter homeplace, precipitating eruptions of pulse-racing drama.

Between this and the noise and the riffraffy behaviors by some of the circus employees, the townies became disenchanted with the wintering arrangements. The presence of the circus, through their winter hiatus, had definitely kicked up the coin in the city strongbox thanks to the spending of circus folks locally, the outlays made on materials for repairs, replacements and general gussying up of costumes and gear, and by the spreading around of cash on the part of visitors drawn to Venice by the circus.

With the 101 Wild West Show, the Al G. Barnes Circus produced a Valentine's ball that raised oodles for community charities. It provided animals and humans for Kinney's annual New Years Eve parades and for the parade in celebration and gratitude at the ending of World War I. Yet still came the point when the influence of financial enhancement no longer held sway.

And so – in 1920 – Barnes purchased 120 acres of land on Washington Boulevard between Venice and Culver City for his band of astonishments' new winter quarters. Just seven years later the population of the area had grown exponentially with people who didn't like the circus as a neighbor instigating another move, to Baldwin Park this time.

The American Circus Corporation purchased the Al G. Barnes Circus in 1929 for a million dollars. That very same year it was further swallowed up into the Ringling Brothers & Barnum & Bailey Circus. Al G. Barnes, himself, inconspicuously sallied off into the sunset.

He died in 1931.

Chapter 7

a movie minx in venice

She was petite and pretty with a great mass of dark hair and large dark eyes and from her tomboy days back on Staten Island Mabel Normand was still athletic and agile. For the summer months she maintained her own cottage in Venice and during the rest of the year she scooted out each Sunday to swim in the Pacific and hang out with her silent film friends, Roscoe "Fatty" Arbuckle and his wife Minta Durfee. They had a home right down on the beach and spread Japanese tablecloths on the sand, around which their group would gather to picnic, chatter and cut-up.

One day, as Mabel was returning from her spin in the surf they could see there was something with her. That "something" turned out to be a dolphin, which joined her as she swam back from the pier. People didn't know much about dolphins in those days but our Mabel was fearless and simply flung her arm around it. Every Sunday after that, for nearly a year, she and the dolphin paddled among the ocean waves together, as happily as a pair of sea otter sisters. Then one Sunday it just stopped showing up.

Mabel Normand came to California in 1912 to make ditzy movies in the sunshine in the company of her boyfriend Mack Sennett, head of the Keystone Film Company, and a squad of demented deliverers of thoroughly madcap mayhem. In just the first year they created 140 short, lunatic laugh fests.

Mabel set the bar for slapstick finesse and zany comedienne antics, often expressed with an underlying quality of tenderness. Due to her background as an artists' model rather than as a stage actress, she possessed an instinctual grasp of performing for the camera, keeping her movements subtle, or as subtle as a

25

movement can be when conveying a good swift kick, pitching a pie in the face, or receiving one.

With its beach, lagoon, canals, the amusement zone attractions and Mediterranean architecture, Venice was a favorite all-purpose location for making movies. Mabel was in several made here: *The Water Nymph, Mabel's New Hero, Fatty & Mabel Adrift* and most importantly to film making history, *Tillie's Punctured Romance*, the hilarious first feature-length comedy ever filmed. Its wild wind-up was shot at the Abbot Kinney pier.

Though undocumented, it's conceptually sound and one might presume with confidence that Mabel was repeatedly and gleefully whooshed about on Venice's behemoth Race Through the Clouds rollercoaster. She *did* keep a summer home here, remember, and she had a reputation as a thrill seeker. Equally, being a reckless connoisseuse of speed, it is practically unthinkable that Mabel would have missed the Venice St. Patrick's Day Grand Prix won by her buddy Barney Oldfield, with whom she made the movie *Barney Oldfield's Race for a Life* a couple years before.

Mabel and Mack were definitely special guests at a surprise birthday event got up for the "Father of the Western," screenwriter/producer/director Thomas Ince, at the Venice Country Club. Most of the 300 guests were from Ince's own studio. The affair consisted of a sumptuous banquet, dancing and impromptu entertainments, lasting till after 4:00 a.m.

She was known to hang out – sometimes dancing a torrid tango in the arms of Charlie Chaplin – at the classy Ship Café (a.k.a. the Cabrillo) where handsome waiters, fetchingly got up as Spanish naval officers from the 1500s, served up epicurean pleasures. As dishy queen to Ince Studio star Barney Sherry's handsome king, Mabel was radiant in a new Paris frock at the head of the grand march opening a glitzy Thanksgiving ball held at the Venice Dance Pavilion.

She was already familiar with tooling about in electriquettes from her making of movies at the 1915 Panama-California Exposition in San Diego and the Panama-Pacific International Exposition that same year in San Francisco, for which they were designed. When the two-passenger motorized wicker chairs became available to rent for trundling up and down the promenade between Venice and Santa Monica, Mabel – this time in the company of aviator Walter Brookins – was tapped to demonstrate their use. She was also employed in ads seen in the *Venice Vanguard* touting the availability of the jazzy new boardwalk transporters.

Not only was she a well-known habitué of Venice, Mabel Normand and Venice were really rather alike. Both were famed, fun, lively, inimitable. And both brought joy to thousands at a time.

Chapter 8

road race

What do you do when you have a perfectly good measured track left over after a rousing St. Patrick's Day grand prix road race won by the mega-flamboyant, cigar chomping Barney Oldfield? If you're the city fathers of Venice, California in the spring of 1915 you simply roll out another ripping race – on motorcycles this time – to cover the very same ground. After all, the streets had already been widened, regraded, resurfaced. Out of caution, trees, streetlamps, power lines and the railroad station were relocated.

In Venice speed and daring were taken seriously.

Prior to this time, road race events typically took place between two cities located some hundreds of miles from one another. Condensing the venue intensified the thrill. The 3.1-mile Venice track was a triangulated affair whipping along Washington Boulevard to Rose Avenue to Compton Road – now Lincoln Boulevard – then returning to Washington Boulevard. Ninety-seven laps equaled 300 miles.

To crank up the quickness factor, banked wooden curves connected the long concrete straightaways. They were constructed from 2x4s rescued from the rubble left by the 1913 fire that destroyed the circular, 20-degree banked Los Angeles Motordrome in nearby Playa del Rey. Built in 1910 it was the first high-banked board speedway in the world and facilitated racers in reaching truly hair-raising speeds.

The promoter of the race was a master motorcyclist himself. Christened with the telling moniker "Daredevil," Paul Derkum's creds were everlastingly confirmed in 1908 when he set ten new world records in a single gritty day on the one-mile dirt track at Agricultural Park in Los Angeles. Five years – and countless races

– later the Daredevil prevailed in the maiden running of the ruthless 421-mile San Diego to Phoenix Desert Race that pitted the riders, not just against one another, but against sand and rock slides, dry washes, sunstroke and gun wielding Mexican bandits.

The showdown billed as the Grand Prize International Motorcycle Race at Venice was rescheduled from March 28th to Easter Sunday, April 4th due to rain, giving time for a couple more seasoned champs to blow in from Kansas, culminating in a field of thirty-seven, astride their motorized mounts, in an extreme of concentrated contention.

Both factory sponsored and independents, some were on Excelsiors or Indians or Cyclones – the real heavy hitters in the realm of motorcycle muscle. Some were on rides of less formidable repute. Four of them were on Harley-Davidsons.

In business twelve years, Harley-Davidson focused on rugged reliability – earth hugging flight not so much – and had already won favor with a whole plethora of police departments. But for the purpose of selling motorcycles there was nothing to compare with winning races. Harking to this factoid they rolled out a newly designed engine and a team of experienced riders, including Leslie "Red" Parkhurst and Otto Walker. Only 19, Parkurst had been riding and winning for six years. Team Captain Walker was the amateur Western Federation of Motorcyclists title-holder before going pro the year before.

At half past noon, that Easter Sunday, the palpable excitement was stoked even higher by warm up acts that were legitimate events in themselves: Barney Oldfield tearing through fast laps in the Bugatti he would drive in the Indy 500 followed by a few scorching laps by Paul Derkum.

When the official flag finally dropped Parkhurst and Walker instantly leapt into the lead – and remained there for the duration. With never more than a few feet between them they were all but Siamese twins upon their blazing Harleys as they hurtled around the course well ahead of all the rest, on stock machines, unlike most which had been customized for racing action.

For 270 miles Parkhurst was just slightly out front; in the end, after an edgy 4 hours, 24 minutes and 17-1/5 seconds at a record-setting average speed of 68-97/100 miles per hour, Otto Walker claimed Harley's first national win. Parkhurst was just 15-3/5 seconds behind him.

Walker would replicate his victory three months later at another 300-mile road race in Dodge City. In the coming years he would go on to other triumphs, not least of which as the first winning rider in a motorcycle race embracing an average speed over 100 miles per hour.

As a capturer of cash for city coffers Venice's 1915 Grand Prize International Motorcycle Race was a flop, as was the St. Patrick's Day motorcar race. As a Harley-Davidson legend launcher it was outstanding. And just the beginning of Harley's thundering presence in Venice.

Chapter 9

infectious tsunami

It was the greatest health disaster in all of history, more lethal – given its far shorter run – than the 14th century's plague to which it is often compared. It crashed over continents like killer tsunamis and before it was over it caused fifty to a hundred million people to forevermore be spoken of in the past tense.

They perished, sometimes, at practically the speed of sound. One chronicle tells of four women playing bridge till late one night; by morning three of them were dead. Due to the operative mechanism of the virus, which pitched the immune system into a suffocating, macrophage-multiplying frenzy, the most endangered were healthy young adults. The more vigorous the immune system, the more psycho it went, so it seemed.

Usually referred to as the Swine Flu or Spanish Flu, the 1918 influenza pandemic didn't skip Venice, California. During the initial stages of the malady, county health officials adopted the same prescriptive assumed when masses of sickly consumptives crowded into to SoCal in the 1880s: namely the magic of the area's salubrious sunshine. As the flu peril increased, Venice city fathers undertook so-called sanitizing saltwater wash-ups of its streets every day, advertising the hyper-optimistic prophylaxis via half-page proclamations in the *Los Angeles Times*. Similarly, a well-respected physician, in all apparent seriousness, issued dubious prevention tips like "excitement should be avoided by all means."

In October 1918, Venice was as bereft of jolliness as everywhere else. Absent was the lively bustle of ride-tenders, barkers, and crowds of larking day-trippers customary during Southern California's affable autumn months. In its place remained an eerily surrealistic near-ghost town and a wafting stench of disinfectant.

33

Those who were out and about sported gauze surgical masks and were decidedly on-task, moving forth with purpose and keeping their distance from anyone else that was out there. Schools, movie theatres, churches, dance halls, restaurants, saloons and other such enclosed public venues were ordered to close by Venice City officials.

Directives were posted calling for the avoidance of coughers and sneezers and people who spit, of crowds and dusty rooms. They also instructed: stop smoking, drink loads of water, don't overeat and "keep your bowels open" – whatever that means.

Endowed with authority and outfitted with red armbands, hazard suggesting helmets and powerful flashlights, Venice Quarantine Patrols were dispatched. They swooped through the neighborhoods stopping at each household, ordering those families failing a health test confined to their homes and posting bright green notices of warning on their doors. Quarantining, it is now agreed, was an efficacious practice; and the gaping lack of health care facilities in Venice produced the serendipitous benefit of aiming the afflicted elsewhere.

For many who survived, the ailment's exiting swansong was violent, involuntary spasms of the diaphragm and respiratory organs – a.k.a. hiccups – occasionally persisting for weeks. Tales from this time of calamity include opportunistic bandits who made use – to commit robberies – of the prevalent and therefore unnoticeable disguise offered by the protective gauze masks; and of children skipping rope and chanting with gothic insouciance:

> *I had a little bird*
> *Its name was Enza*
> *I opened the window*
> *And in-flu-enza*

Venetian Earl Pyle had a parrot, which mimicked his influenza induced coughing with such crazy-making exactitude that Pyle popped the bird in a cage and hung it out on the porch. From this perch its faux coughing sent passersby running, perversely affording Pyle a good giggle.

Part of the Al G. Barnes Circus then hibernating for the season in Venice and bizarrely diagnosed with influenza, Wally the orang-utan was to be seen waddling about on the pier and boardwalk, led on a leash by one of the circus' trained dogs, sanguinely soaking up sunbeams for reinvigoration.

By the end of December the epidemic had abated sufficiently for Abbot Kinney to throw his annual kids' Christmas bash, for which the dance pavilion became a scene of enchantment. At the center of the awesome glitteration rose a twenty-foot, lovingly ornamented tree beneath which were mountains of colorfully wrapped gifts for all the children, bags of candies and stockings stuffed with juicy blood oranges from Kinney's Sierra Madre ranch, Kinneloa. There was a parade and a feast and lots of cheery entertainments; later a spectacular fireworks show on the pier.

A New Year's celebration went forward too, albeit with a ban on confetti, which, it was feared, might cause truly life-threatening sneezes.

With these, finally, a returning sense of normalcy began to gradually settle over Venice.

the guy from villa city

William Carroll's a raconteur of a very high order. At 95 his memory is still as sharp as crocodile teeth and he possesses a vast plethora of dynamic life tales that he spins out with breezy panache, investing his stories with a nifty, almost swashbuckling air.

He tells of spending five months slogging along on the incomplete Pan-American Highway between Juarez Mexico and Panama City on a BSA motorcycle. His yarns about test driving and consulting for the auto industries of both the United States and Europe include instigation of the cross breeding between the Sunbeam Alpine and Carroll Shelby's Cobra, resulting in the Sunbeam Tiger. He was one of the first photographers to capture 19-year-old Norma Jean Dougherty's — soon to be Marilyn Monroe's — mesmerizing effect on a camera lens, part of a collection of Monroe images brought together in June 2010 for a glittering, historic exhibition at the Andrew Weiss Gallery in Beverly Hills.

His boyhood in Venice made an admirable apprenticeship for all his blitzing about, living life to its fullest. He was not much more than a toddler when his mother assumed management of Villa City, the eucalyptus-tree-veiled, sprawling tent complex tucked up next to the Grand Canal.

Having twigged to the fact that the number of completed hotel rooms would be inadequate to accommodate the anticipated crowds that would rush to the opening of Venice-of-America in July of 1905, Abbot Kinney called into being a tent city in the nature of those already existing on Santa Catalina and Coronado islands. As luxury lodgings caught up with the need, the tents became available for tourists of more modest means, then in 1914 as small apartmenty rentals for some of Venice's working class.

In her soon-to-be-published novel, *Lions and Gondolas*, Laura Shepard Townsend describes one of Kinney's tent cottages, circa 1918, as "a villa in white canvas, sturdy on a wooden platform, and cushioned with woven carpets from the Orient...we had electrical lamps and a refrigerator ... and gas fueled the heater to make our tent cozy... The white enamel stove danced flames at the touch of a match. It even had a built-in steel griddle for Mother's delicious buttermilk pancakes. Supposedly we were camping out, but our bed mattresses were thickly padded, and supplied with clean, soft cotton linens every week."

There were 246 little canvas abodes in Villa City; the manager's living quarters were nicer and more spacious. A grocery store, a recreation center, laundry facilities and its own free lending library occupied the compound as well.

Next door to Bill lived a little girl – Sara – and they came to be fine mentors to one another on the subjects of anatomy and physiology. There were plenty of other young male rascals too, who made commendable cohorts in Carroll's full-time practice of running amok.

In the company of such sidekicks he embarked on swell – though not necessarily well considered – adventures. One day they could be found shinnying along the big sewer pipe that ran directly beneath the pier for about a quarter-mile over the ocean, risking utter doom at any moment; or more tamely, bent-pin-and-soggy-bread fishing from a Venice Italy-inspired pedestrian bridge spanning the Grand Canal. On another day they might amuse themselves tossing tomatoes at passing cars, or surfing with his mother's ironing board or – 35-feet above the ground – scaling parapets from one building to the next to slither along the rooftop of the aerial walkway that connected the St. Marks Hotel's two separate sections.

The sad day came when Carroll arrived home from school to find all the scene-setting eucalyptus trees that had surrounded Villa City – with their stringy bark and their flowing, fragrant leaves – lying across the street, cut down in the name of progress, Abbot Kinney no longer alive to protect them. In the fall of 1927 the tent cottages were emptied and demolished so that, within their absence, a new – though ultimately unrealized – business district could arise.

"Venice was the most exciting place a boy could grow up," Bill Carroll contends. "A narrow-gage, steam-powered miniature train encircled the town, providing ready transport. We had the beach, we had the huge plunge; we had two movie theatres – the Neptune and the Criterion – and a pier just full of things: Three roller coasters, the Giant Dipper, a haunted ship, the Ship Café, and a fun house with rides and slides."

"Now – how could it get better than that?" he asks.

Chapter 11

the bodacious bungalow

They were almost as common to the Venice, California geography as the seagulls on its beach. Expressions of Arts and Crafts philosophies, they sprung up all over the country, but wherever they were they were called *California* bungalows for this was, indeed, their native habitat.

Egalitarian as chicken eggs, they came in high class, middle class and do-it-yourselfer varieties: from the Greene and Greene designed masterwork Gamble house in Pasadena, to the passels of build-by-number homes in Venice that were sold by the Ready-Cut Bungalow Company or Sears Roebuck.

The less upscale were disparaged as "speculator driven," by architect Charles Greene, but the bungalow was well-loved by all manner of folk, due in part to prodigious proselytizing by bungalow evangelists in national magazines like the *Ladies Home Journal* and *House Beautiful*, as well as more specialized periodicals such as *Craftsman* or *American Bungalow*.

Their popularity peaked during the 1920s, but the most prototypical examples of the form were built before World War I. Innovative in their provision of stylishly progressive digs to even the average homeowner, they were habitable icons of the American Dream oozing the salubrious SoCal spirit – from its casual lifestyle to its outdoorsy nature – that in Venice was undertaken with passionate gusto. In addition, bungalows were considered a celebration of family, an institution that was viewed by some as endangered in those early years of the twentieth century, due to the "new woman" and suffragist movements.

Nestled amongst sun-soaked gardens, in their quintessential manifestations the bungalows seemed to rise up organically from their surroundings. Low and horizontal, they were generally one story – except for some of the high-end architect-designed homes – their linear configuration harkening back to the early California Spanish ranchos.

Typically, the exterior walls were redwood, natural or stained shakes or dark stained clapboard, with window sashes and bargeboard along the eaves painted white. The homes' gently pitched roofs extended beyond the walls to rest on tapered posts – usually of stone or cement – creating cozy front porches. Sometimes they embraced pueblo or Spanish revival forms. Sometimes they exhibited a Japanese air. Colorful awnings might top the windows investing the dwelling with a jaunty pizzazz.

Inside, the living room flowed gracefully through an arch and into the dining room, creating an impression of greater grandeur. Masculine in affect, their dark paneled walls were accented by mission-finished woodwork. Ceiling beams conveyed a satisfying sense of hominess and plate rails placed 18" below the ceiling continued the sensation of linearity. There were open stone fireplaces with broad mantles, built-in sideboards and the little snuggeries with cushion-covered benches known as inglenooks. Mission-style and Gustav Stickly-designed furniture were congenial with the interior design and mirrors visually expanded the spaces and added light.

In contrast to the living and dining rooms, the rest of the home was painted white. The small, step-saving kitchen presented zinc-topped counters and the new fashioned ship-like built-ins. Filled with mechanical gadgets it functioned as the housewife's own little factory in which nutritious meals were efficiently turned out in promotion of her family's well-being. Off the kitchen, a hall led to a bath and two bedrooms in the most common versions. The bathrooms were a triumph of modern plumbing and porcelain. The frequent use of disappearing beds increased the utility of the bedrooms.

Bungalows begat bungalow courts reminiscent of religious camps. The first, St. Francis Court was built in Pasadena in 1909 as lodging for well-to-do tourists wintering in Southern California's agreeable clime. Some of the snazzier hotels put up their own bungalow courts on hotel grounds. Bungalow courts led to motels, then bungalow court apartments featuring parallel rows or U-shaped arrangements of tiny homes laid down around a community garden, like a friendly neighborhood of dollhouses.

A fabulous linking of function to form, the idea of a bungalow in the California sun sang out to the salivating residents of other places, filling them with delicious desire. Bungalow postcards sent by friends or family added a frenzy of fuel to the fantasies. To further tantalize the smitten, California fruit might arrive in crates festooned with colorful lithographic labels boasting bodacious bungalows. The seductive images simmered in a tasty motivational stew, ultimately prompting swarms of California dreamers to go west.

These many decades later the charming bungalows still hold sway in Venice neighborhoods as much-coveted abodes.

aimee goes missing

It was a nice day at the beach on May 18, 1926, the day Aimee Semple McPherson waded into the Venice surf and vanished.

Sister Aimee was an evangelist with a genius for religion as theatre sharpened by her years on the tent revival circuit. Once widowed, once divorced, she'd tooled around the country with her children and mother – a gypsy with a bible preaching and saving and healing; till 1919 when she arrived in Los Angeles and recognized it as her spirit's true home. By 1923 she had built – and paid for – Angelus Temple, a circular church across from Echo Park accommodating 5300 zealous worshipers at a setting, three of them each Sunday plus one on Wednesday evenings.

Flamboyant and glamorous, McPherson favored slinky white robes and marcelled hair, and storming to the pulpit on a motorcycle was just one of the bits of shtick she employed to keep the attention of the congregants riveted and ready to receive her message of God's love. Within just a year she added a bible college and radio station to her repertoire. These were followed in the Great Depression by a comprehensive social service agency providing food, clothing, rent money and medical assistance to the needy.

Declaring she needed a break, she and her secretary hauled themselves out to Venice Beach, on that May afternoon in 1926, checking into a second floor suite overlooking the Pacific at the Ocean View Hotel. Out on the sand, the secretary was left reclining in the sun as McPherson plunged into the waves. She failed to return from that swim.

Keening and praying and vigiling, Aimee's adorers filled the beach for weeks. Her mother dropped armloads of lilies from a plane onto the sea; one of the distraught committed suicide. At the same time a massive search for her or her body was undertaken in which two of her would-be rescuers died. Surrendering to what seemed to be so, on June 20th a daylong memorial for McPherson was held at Angelus Temple; three days later she wandered unharmed out of an Arizona border town. What had already been one of the biggest news stories of the decade, now took on the sweet, seductive scent of the salacious.

Her family and fans rejoiced wildly in her apparent resurrection. The police, however, were struck by the fact that when last seen she was wearing a green bathing suit while on her reappearance she was conventionally clad – right down to a respectable corset. The soles of the shoes that had supposedly stumbled across miles of desert were undamaged, and her face showed no sign of sunburn.

McPherson claimed she had been kidnapped, carried off to a shack in northern Mexico and tortured. But Kenneth Ormiston, the married – though separated – former engineer at her radio station, had also gone missing and it was discovered that he had checked into a cottage at Carmel-by-the-Sea in the company of a woman simply seething similarity to Sister Aimee.

Law enforcement officials were pitched into a huff by the whole affair, convening a grand jury and going to trial over McPherson's offence to public morals. She stood firm and with unflappable defiance she announced, "That's my story and I'm sticking to it."

Whatever the "truth" of this melodrama, for the passionate woman who so loved God and cared about people, celebrity had become a golden cage, confining her to loneliness amidst the crowds. The misadventure culminated in fizzled judicial proceedings that left the grand jury, D.A.'s office, a police captain and a judge looking silly.

Sometime later she would visit the prosecuting D.A. in prison himself where he languished for his own legal faux pas. The three deaths haunted the rest of her life.

During the 1970s, when the Ocean View Hotel was refurbished to take up a new function as apartments for low-income old folks, the writer Collette's pithy philosophy was emblazoned over the elevators: "You will do foolish things, but do them with enthusiasm," perhaps an homage to Aimee. Though not open to the public for a time, the building at the corner of Ocean Front Walk and Rose Avenue has recently been reinvented as AIR Venice, Luxury Oceanfront Accommodations for "hip beachfront living."

Chapter 13

desperate dancing

During the madcap Roaring Twenties marathon dancing gurgled up from the same pond of goofy high spirits that spewed forth such dippy activities as flagpole sitting, competitive egg-eating, endurance kissing and swallowing goldfish. In the U.S., 32-year old dance teacher Alma Cummings got the dance marathon craze underway in March of 1923 when she beat out the competition at a New York City ballroom after 27 hours of non-stop dancing – wearing out six young men and several pairs of shoes as she did so.

Kicked up a few notches, by 1928 dance marathons were decidedly theatrical affairs. The new model was about making money. Packaged like a beauty pageant, the promoters arranged for the facility and its appropriate spiffing up to accommodate their show – a cinchy task in Venice given its pre-existing Sunset Ballroom and the Venice Dancehall.

Promoters put up the prize money and publicized zealously to attract the teeming host of spectators that would make the whole enterprise lucrative. They laid on the help, from the glib Masters of Ceremony and dance bands, to the floor judges, the nurses and food providers. They processed the amateur entrants and also engaged drop-in entertainment, like local celebrities, vaudeville acts, singers, exhibition dancers and the clandestine marathon-dancing professionals to spark confrontations and keep the mood lively.

Executing – when fresh – the turkey trot, Texas Tommy, fox-trot, bunny hug and tango, less grace than grit was required of the participants who often were drawn to the contests, according to one Freudian psychologist, by neurotic complexes lusting after

a refreshing attention fix. For some of the Venice marathon contestants – more so than for those in St. Louis or Minneapolis, say
– the competitions additionally held out the hope, far-fetched to
be sure, of being discovered by a slumming Hollywood producer
and instantaneously turned into a star.

The Great Depression years saw dance marathons harden into
something quite dodgy, coming to be – as they did – a vehicle
of survival rather than just playful hilarity. They were grueling,
months-long, fortitude-busting trials that went on 24-hours a
day with only a ten to fifteen minute break per hour in which to
eat, sleep and tend to one's toilette. Contestants suffered blisters,
swelling, muscle spasms, anguish, debilitation, hallucinations,
heart attacks or worse, but for the duration of one's stamina there
was the assurance of something to eat, a roof over one's head, a
cot upon which to lie down, if only for moments.

Already in possession of a certain sleazy insalubrity, Venice
was an apt and popular venue for the sordid Depression era
dance marathons. Though somewhat less vile than public hang-
ings or wrestling matches between Christians and lions, paying
customers cheerfully coughed up 25-cents apiece for the perverse
pleasure of watching the dissipated stumblings and staggerings
of the exhausted competitors; the staged or the spontaneous bits
of drama; the flashes of violence, as they occurred within the
patriotic bunting-draped dancehall.

Published in 1935, *They Shoot Horses Don't They?* is the story
of one such marathon, staged by a crew of opportunistic promoters whose earnest idea of high-class amusement was the public
wedding of one of the couples. The author was Horace McCoy
who had worked as a beachside marathon bouncer, allowing him
to saturate his tale with a tawdry authenticity gleaned from up-
close observation.

It's not a breezy read. The chapters open with the hours
elapsed and the number of contestants still remaining, fueling an
oppressive sense of inevitable doom; while below the pier the surf
swims – in and out, in and out – echoing the demented circularity
of the movement in the ballroom above. The central characters,
Robert and Gloria, like the other marathon couples – indeed, like
those in real life – are trapped between the mercilessness of the

times, the perpetual-motion freak show in which they themselves are prime attractions and the posse of self-righteous moralists crusading against the marathons, one of few options their cruel situation affords.

The novel is a triumph of existential joylessness, just as the marathons had become. The 1969 Jane Fonda movie version, shot in the Aragon Ballroom on Venice's Lick Pier, is equally depressing.

In the mid-1930s the form fell out of favor on account of widening impoverishment and boredom on the part of the marathon audience.

Chapter 14

oil

They were gathered together, a whole crackpot grove of grubby towers, uglifying the once lovely shoreline, fouling sand and surf and the toes that might touch them with despicable tar-y blobs. The wells sprung up, too, in private yards in Venice, like bad-smelling lawn statuary, appallingly bereft of beauty but providing of welcome income, thereby engorging 95% of the residents with an eager-beaver impatience to despoil their own nests.

Maybe the response would have been more measured had the discovery of Venice oil – on December 18, 1929 – not followed so closely upon the catastrophic crash of the Wall Street Stock Market less than two months before, sending the formerly-successful swan diving out of the windows of tall buildings, irretrievably ushering in the Great Depression.

The motivation was set in motion, one might say, in 1897 when then-17-year old Earle C. Anthony built the first automobile in Los Angeles that sent him scooting around town at up to six miles per hour. From this vehicular genesis the car population grew exponentially. By 1909 the city of L.A. nailed down the bragging rights to the greatest number of automobiles per capita of any city in the world.

The gasoline to power those autos was mostly sold in 5-gallon cans out of drug and grocery stores. In 1912, Anthony had another brilliant brain fugue and like some auspiciously re-articulated Johnny Appleseed began ambitiously spreading canopy-covered fueling stations along the California roadways. SoCal's unquenchable thirst for oil was well underway – as was the drilling to slake its thirst inaugurated by Edward L. Doheny, using picks and shovels and a sharpened eucalyptus tree trunk, near the current site of Dodger Stadium.

The Ohio Oil Company was the oil-finding functionary of Standard Oil. Weirdly enough, its maiden discovery attempt in Venice was focused on land abutting the chi-chi residential neighborhood east of the Grand Canal at Avenue 35. As if it had just been waiting for a petroleum seeker to come along and hit it with a refreshing Heimlich maneuver, the earth promptly coughed up black treasure – and just as swiftly Venetians went wonky with oil fever.

Verily, as oil fields go, it proved to be a rather puny puddle and between its feeble volume and its rampant over-drilling the boom played out with a relative quickness.

That first ambiance altering well produced 3000 barrels of oil per day – initially – others up to 5000 barrels daily. Nine months after the original strike, there were fifty wells pumping for the Standard Oil brand in Venice – as well as that of other major oil companies – creating weekly Depression-era paydays for hundreds, boosting the rank of the Del Rey field to the sixth largest oil field in the state.

But the beach was corrupted; an elementary school was closed, its students dispersed for their safety. An explosion obliterated one of the rigs and the swoony, upscale neighborhood was a mess.

At the end of 1930 there were 148 wells giving up almost 47,000 barrels of oil each day; by the next year, 450 wells were producing. In 1932 there was a great slacking off. Many of the wells were depleted; production of the others was plummeting.

Sadly, "when you're dead, lie down," was not a philosophy that would come into play here. Rather, it would be a decades long process of ever-diminishing returns and revolting drilling waste that continued to pollute the waterways and poison the land. On top of which, Venice was being steadily stiffed by the City of Los Angeles for obligatory royalties due it – according to the Coastal Tidelands Trust – to offset the damages which rained down on the exploited area like some monstrous torrential typhoon.

Equally alarming for L.A.'s redheaded stepchild, in the 1960s the City kept trying to promote *new* drilling for oil in Venice, finally prevailing with a slant-drilled, offshore well. To soothe the outraged, its ugly derrick was tricked out as a lighthouse then garnished with attractive landscaping. The whole time Venice's supposedly guaranteed share of the proceeds was brazenly redirected to fund a fishing pier in nearby San Pedro.

Another clear case of oil well abuse.

Chapter 15

a life beside the bay

Her brain bubbles over with uncontainable memories of her tenure in Venice, which began a year after her birth in 1929. The self-delighting stream cascades like white water to churn up – in just minutes – a torrent of random recollections: Venice High School half-up half-down on the day following the 1933 Long Beach earthquake that clobbered a fair bit of the Los Angeles milieu, the Rattle Snake Museum on the pier, Bobby Kennedy campaigning in Venice in 1968 for the Democratic party's nomination for President of the United States.

Dolores Montgomery is a compulsive storyteller with an evangelist's zeal for yarning about Venice, in its many moods and manifestations. "When we're born we're lucky. When we turn one year old we're even luckier," she declares, "if our parents decide to move to an unknown Westside Los Angeles area called Venice" – in far off California.

Here her family was the first settled into a home on Ashwood Avenue across from the brick Venice High School with its statue out front featuring film star Myrna Loy – before she *was* Myrna Loy. It was an iconic Spanish style home with a red-tile roof. Directly to the north was a vastness of lima bean fields farmed by Japanese eternally beset by bean-loving gophers. Around 1950 both bean fields and neighborhood would whimsically transmute into Mar Vista.

Whatever other role she assumed – X-ray tech, launcher of the Head Start Program in Venice, producer of slick auto shows held at Loyola Marymount University, or an Air Force executive secretary with top security clearance – Montgomery always found additional ways to make contributions to her community. She even received a beautiful framed resolution for her good works.

Since 1992 bone-shattering osteoporosis has kept her foot pretty much nailed to the floor – so to speak – at a nursing home over in Culver City. Though bed-bound she still does what she can, including narrating the quirky history of the hometown she loves so that it's not sucked into the mists of oblivion.

Decorated with her own delicious little drawings, this local treasure wrote a series of memory pieces for the Heal the Bay organization's volunteer newsletter, *Sea Stars*. Sometimes cheery, sometimes poignant, in lively, evocative prose she remembered surfers and lifeguards, a seal being hauled off in a police car – like some common criminal – after days of trying to keep it off Pacific Coast Highway. She remembered the blackouts and terrifying air raid sirens during World War II, and she remembered the time the bulls ran.

I am not certain of the year (1999?) but two men stopped their truck, in which they were transporting live bulls, to eat lunch in Venice. Some curious kids decided to release the animals from their confinement, and they swung the truck doors open, which sent 10-15 puzzled bulls scrambling onto Lincoln Boulevard, past Lake Street to Beethoven. To everyone's surprise, the LAPD put together a posse of officers who went after them, whirling ropes, corralling the bulls and bringing most of them down. One evaded them, however, and made it all the way to Main Street, where it drew a crowd that gathered around him, looking at his sad eyes, feeling sorry for his predicament.

Her captivating stories and beguiling personality enchanted readers and generated stacks fan mail. Montgomery's editor, Gabriele Morgan, observed that "Her bemused perspective, even when recounting painful personal passages in her life, allowed readers to feel they were seeing a kind of time-lapse vision of the Santa Monica/Venice/Mar Vista and Marina areas as she put her recollections into context with the current landscape, literally and also sentimentally as longtime-touchstones such as the red cars and entertainment piers in Venice, Ocean Park and Santa Monica vanished beneath the waves of time."

For Dolores Montgomery, those images of yesteryear just keep showing up on the screen of her mind, images such as: the doggie-shaped hamburger joint on Washington Boulevard, the floods and Mardi Gras celebrations in Venice during the 1930s, John Travolta and Olivia Newton-John filming the movie *Grease* in 1978 at Venice High.

Montgomery's head-pictures of the past run in a sweet, endless loop: cherished vignettes of a life beside the bay.

Chapter 16

*of sweet dreams &
sandcastles*

From the very beginning there was a Japanese presence in Venice, California. Planted on the Abbot Kinney pier, it took the form of a Japanese Pavilion and was a stunning expression of Kinney's admiration for that culture. Passing beneath an oriental gateway entwined with twin dragons, lanterns and colored lights, one entered the pavilion and was swept into an enchantment of unfamiliar scents, sounds and sights, to lap up a sample of the lifeway, to make purchases from exotic offerings, to take refreshments in the teahouse.

Alternately, those self-same scents, sounds and sights may have been like a lamp in a window to those of Japanese ancestry seeking a new homeplace. Most were farmers or fishermen, many made homeless by the 1906 earthquake and fire in San Francisco. Others simply drifted over from Los Angeles.

They were the *Issei*: the first generation of Japanese who had been born in Japan and immigrated to the United States, becoming resident aliens. They embraced this new land – new life – at the other side of the Pacific, entrusting it with their dreams for a better life, laboring diligently to bring them to fruition. The *Niesi* were the equally hard-working American born offspring of the *Issei*.

They found in Venice an experience of plenty. The sea gave up bountiful harvests to the fishermen; the soil was rich, the bright Southern California sun ameliorated by the by the cool morning fog's soft caress produced for the farmers excellent crops of celery, lima beans, gardenias. Successful restaurants and other establishments bore names such as Osaka or Nagasaki.

In 1921 the Venice-Palms Industrial Association – essentially a farmers' guild – was founded. In the next few years, a judo studio and a Japanese language school were established. Other organizations for cultural preservation, recreation and enrichment would follow, all ultimately part of the Venice Japanese Community Center on Braddock Drive.

But it wasn't all sweet times and sushi. Vile anti-Japanese attitudes were afoot causing the withholding of citizenship, the disallowance of property ownership, sometimes inducing violent confrontations. The apogee of anti-Japanese practices was reached following the bombing of Pearl Harbor and the U.S. entry into World War II, when President Franklin D. Roosevelt signed Executive Order 9066, an order that rolled over lives like waves over sandcastles. Kicking the concept of due process to the curb, it summarily committed 110,000 men, women and children of Japanese descent – two-thirds of them American citizens – to various internment camps.

Given only a matter of days to make whatever desperate arrangements possible for their properties, businesses and possessions, the Japanese Venetians were ordered to gather, with only what they could carry, on April 25, 1942 at Venice and Lincoln Boulevards where they waited with quiet dignity in a long, long line before being hauled off by the busload to Manzanar, 230 miles northeast of L.A., high in the Sierra Nevada Mountains.

Encircled with barbed wire and guarded by submachine gun armed military police in eight towers surrounding its perimeter, they arrived at the camp consisting of rows of barracks – glorified chicken coops, really – flung together in a hasty, slapdash fashion to house the 10,046 internees. Compensated at a rate of $8.00 to $19.00 per month the prisoners were expected to maintain the compound. Despite the injustice, the loss, the profound disillusionment they took up their employment with resolute purpose.

As well as farmers and fishermen, there were engineers, architects, teachers, nurses, artists and writers. Though their "apartments," separated by fabric walls, were tiny and primitive and offered no privacy, and there were communal latrines and a single mess hall, they imposed what comfort they could.

They built schools, a hospital, an auditorium, and places to practice their faith. They created farms, gardens, a pleasure park, and a baseball field. There was a newspaper, a library and a cemetery. There was Kabuki theatre and poetry and dances with swingtime music featuring the "Songbird of Manzanar," Mary Kageyama – recently a Venice High School student. In short, they made of Manzanar a village. Could their eventual leave-taking have not been bittersweet?

At War's end, most of Venice's Japanese residents returned. Many of the families stayed for a while at the Venice Japanese Community Center – temporarily retrofitted as a hostel – before resettling into their own digs. With their usual poise and industry the Japanese of Venice began new lives yet again.

Chapter 17

ray bradbury's venice

Those were the days when the Venice pier
was falling apart and dying in the sea...
Death is a Lonely Business

Ray Bradbury is, of course, most revered for his ingenious fiction of the speculative sort; some of it – most notably *The Martian Chronicles* – was created while he was a resident of Venice between 1941 and 1950. Thirty-five years after decamping, Bradbury transmuted his Venice sojourn into usable history, reclaiming its 1940s milieu as a backdrop for *Death is a Lonely Business,* in which memory is overlaid by mystery.

It was written in homage to writers of the hardboiled school: Dashiell Hammett, Raymond Chandler, James Cain and Ross Macdonald. But it unfolds as languorously, surrealistically, sinuously, as sea kelp vines swaying in the tide and with the goose-pimpling gothic tilt of Edgar Allen Poe.

As a midnight trolley rattles through the rain towards the sea an odiferous but unseen man creeps up behind the tale's teller, the only other occupant of the car, to whisper – chillingly – of death. Less than an hour later the narrator discovers a body floating within an old circus cage submerged in the scummy waters of a Venice canal and he's convinced the two events are connected. In the company of a short, curmudgeony plainclothes detective the sleuthing duly commences.

I typically mow through mystery fiction like a dragon devouring a little covey of hapless peasants. *Death is a Lonely Business* wouldn't allow that. Some of Bradbury's tasty paragraphs I read and read again and again – out loud – to feel his words in my mouth and to revel in the poetry of their sound. His metaphor-charged prose paints oil pumps as pterodactyls, the wood of the dismembered roller coaster as dinosaur bones and he seasons his phrasing with such deliciously pumped up descriptions as that of ideas that "seethed like maggots on a hotplate."

Oddballs and eccentrics swim up from the pages like mermaids and sea serpents and slimy bottom feeders to carry the reader along the strange twists and turns of the narrator's quest. In the guise of Bradbury's own younger self, the storyteller – by contrast – is an innocent, slurping up the peculiar like a hungry aardvark.

My favorite of his motley collection of misfits is Fannie Florianna, a tenderhearted, tenement dwelling past opera diva of hippoesque proportions. She snarfs mayonnaise straight from the jar with a large spoon and keeps a piano box stashed in the alley. "The day I die," she instructs, "bring the piano box up, tuck me in, hoist me down."

Some of the characters and Venice return twice for encores: *A Graveyard for Lunatics* was published in 1990 and *Let's all Kill Constance* in 2003. The trilogy's a demonstration of Ray Bradbury's continuing fondness for this place he once called home, during one of the more inelegant manifestations of its existence.

Though disreputable, to be sure, and blatantly festooned with murders in his fictional versions, Bradbury holds Venice in those times gone by as insouciantly quirky rather than sordid. Some of the book's most bizarre images – like the circus wagons and cages mired in the muck and polluted water of a canal, or the Arabesque mansion on the sand or the false eyeballs displayed upon pedestals in a storefront window – gurgled up from the shabby phantasmagoria that was actually the Venice gestalt in the 1940s. It's a history. Sort of.

The cinema on the pier where the moviegoer could feel the waves roll in and out below as a love story unfolded on the screen was there too. So were the dimly lit trolleys clattering to the sea at midnight, the barbershop fitted with a piano, the faded hand-made sign offering "Canaries for Sale."

This is the place Ray Bradbury has loved from those many decades-ago days when, at noon, he would take time out from his typing to run 100 yards to the surf and jump in for a refreshing swim. This is the place where he first brought his young wife Maggie to live. This is the place that still holds his heart, giving rise to a steadfast support of the Venice Historical Society: in its use of his name on our projects and promotions, in the annual presentations he makes for our meetings and his current leadership in kicking off the restoration fund for the Windward Avenue Colonnades.

For the fabulous tales and the unflinching fidelity: thanks to you, Ray Bradbury.

scott joplin's disciple

Even in a place as well stocked with eccentrics as Venice, Sanford Brunson Campbell stood out as a character. He took up residence in the mid-1920s, then swift as a sunbeam opened a barbershop at 711 Venice Boulevard – next to the Venice City Hall – where he practiced his trade with a distinctive tonsorial technique that crowned his customers with irregular caps of hair that appeared to have been chewed on by a frog.

Apparently haircuts weren't the shop's primary draw.

Brun Campbell was a consummate storyteller. Generously lubricated with exaggeration, embellishment and things he just plain made up, the main thrust of his chronicles was the early years of ragtime – that vibrant musical mode characterized by a strong syncopated melodic line and a regularly accented accompaniment, played chiefly on the piano – and Scott Joplin, the form's preeminent composer, as well as other fine pioneer purveyors of the style. The gist of his story, give or take a few fabrications, went something like this.

Chasing after his dream, in 1899, at the age of 15 Campbell ran away from home and family. Earlier, a day of truancy for the purpose of attending a fair in Oklahoma City led, serendipitously, to an acquaintanceship with Scott Joplin's colleague, Otis Saunders, and an opportunity to play the genre defining "Maple Leaf Rag" from the handwritten, as-yet unpublished manuscript. It commenced a life-long obsession. In this instant of communion Scott Joplin became his idol and ragtime his personal holy grail.

Reaching Sedalia, Missouri – ground zero in the development of ragtime – he caught up with his hero and would later brag (not *quite* factually) that he'd convinced Joplin to take him on as his only white student ever. Campbell was already an accomplished musician but Joplin taught him to play "Maple Leaf Rag" and other Joplin rags precisely as written, with the reverential exactitude one would bring to the playing of a Beethoven sonata: a seriousness in execution seemingly at odds with the spirit of the rollicking music itself.

Christened – maybe *self*-christened – the Ragtime Kid, for several years he flitted around the Midwest, South and Southwest, flashily garbed, playing in saloons and honkytonks, brothels, pool halls and riverboats, in which venues he claimed to have entertained such well-known personalities as Buffalo Bill Cody and Billy the Kid, President Teddy Roosevelt, lawman Bat Masterson, infamous outlaws Frank James, Cole Younger and Emmett Dalton.

Around 1908 he retired from the life of a wandering pianist, married the first of his three wives and followed his dad's footsteps into barbering. His shrewish third wife banned what she called the "trashy" ragtime music from their home and exiled Campbell's piano to his barbershop. Can't think why he took up with this woman!

Hot stuff for a couple of decades, by 1920 ragtime was a fading fashion being replaced in popularity by jazz; but the early 1940s witnessed a revival of the old ragtime music. With an eye to the main chance Brun Campbell promptly rushed in to champion the resurrection. More significant as a carrier than a creator, he made it his mission to spread the gospel of Scott Joplin and the dynamic, original ragtime sound.

For anyone with even a scrap of interest, he was wont to pull the shade, hang a "closed" sign on the barbershop door and hold forth on his favorite topic, or fill the shop with lively, pianoed, ragtime syncopation. A walking, talking primary source, musicologists were on him like pink on a petunia.

He was the subject on radio programs and in numerous books, author and subject in a plethora of articles – including an autobiography – that appeared in such publications as *Jazz Journal*, *The Jazz Record* and *Rag Times*. He lobbied mightily for the filming of a Hollywood biopic about Joplin, made recordings of early ragtime songs – Scott Joplin's "Maple Leaf Rag" among them – producing in the doing something akin to a thrilling time warp.

And he would play just about anyplace, anytime, often at beach area clubs. Campbell might even have been seen as the intermission entertainment at the Aragon Ballroom on Lick Pier while Lawrence Welk and his wholesome band of "champagne music makers" took a break, a fairly schizophrenic juxtaposition of musical philosophies, to be sure.

By the time of his death on November 23, 1952, Sanford Brunson Campbell had achieved a certain celebrity of his own.

miss muscle beach 1948

At 77, all petite and pink and perky and topped by a little halo of spun-sunlight hair, Sara Hirsch Clark may seem – to the non-connoisseur of Muscle Beach lore – an unlikely inductee into the Muscle Beach Hall of Fame. But, there she was this past Labor Day, taking her place amongst other Muscle Beach legends to have been honored in this way including Jack LaLanne, Steve Reeves, Pudgy Stockton and Joe Gold. In recognition, she received a take-homeable Lucite trophy and a bronze plaque bearing her name is now incorporated into the very foundation of Venice's Muscle Beach Weight Pen.

Muscle Beach was born in a children's playground just south of the Santa Monica pier in the mid-1930s, where a bunch of kids started hanging around to practice acrobatics and work out. Gym teacher, Kate Giroux, is credited with kicking it up a few notches by convincing the City and the WPA to install a tumbling platform and to add some rings and parallel bars. The acrobatic beach devotees multiplied, swarming like lemmings to the seaside where they mentored one another in fitness and technique, and before long were joined on weekends by thousands of spectators, thrilled by the free exhibition of their skill.

Disembarking from a West L.A. bus, Sara Clark first came to Muscle Beach on a June day in 1948. She had come to trim down. Just three months later she would be named queen of the realm, a tribute to the concentrated effort it took to so quickly become a lithe maven of hand balancing – a form of gymnastics executed with a partner – and to the personality, poise and stage presence she possessed in such spectacularly copious abundance.

At just four years old she was singing and dancing, Shirley-Temple-moppet-style, for sing-along nights at the Ocean Park Community Center. At eleven Clark was playing the accordion as a USO entertainer. At seventeen she was ripe for her triumph: only the second woman in history to be named Miss Muscle Beach. Following her win, she became a popular subject for magazine articles, appeared in a documentary about Muscle Beach, was a model for Muscle Beach publicity and – in a beauty contest – snagged the title Miss Barbelles.

Many of those long ago, highly visible Muscle Beach regulars felt like misfits in the other areas of their lives. At Muscle Beach they found community and meaning and joy. Muscle Beach became their world and their residencies there were long. It wasn't like that for Sara Clark – she had a gift for fitting in practically anywhere.

As a teen her social calendar was full and at school she was involved in the chorus, modern dance and drama. By the summer of 1949 she was a high school graduate who had matriculated into gainful employment, leaving behind fond memories of her Muscle Beach tenure, to fling herself into all the new experiences to come. She would not return to the Muscle Beach fold until half a century later when she began attending Muscle Beach events in Venice and communing with some of the other Muscle Beach old timers she fell in with while enjoying the competitions – now focusing on bodybuilding rather than the acrobatics of her era.

A dynamic puff of pure energy, Sara Clark moves at warp speed to suck up life with a voracious thirst for each moment. She walks three miles daily, exercises at Curves. She takes acting classes, and ballroom dancing lessons and is a member of a Saturday breakfast bunch called Reel Cowboys. It's a band of Western Film and TV appreciators that, in addition to eating waffles and having fun, raises money in support of the good works of other groups – activity that speaks to Clark's spirit.

These days Sara Clark's grandest passion is volunteering, making life a little better for other folks. She's in training to nurture abused children; a long term volunteer for Meals on Wheels, the Make-A-Wish Foundation, Travelers' Aid at the Los Angeles

Airport and DOLLS (Dedicating Our Loyal Loving Service) in the assistance of people who otherwise fall through the social service cracks.

"Food feeds the tummy, but volunteering feeds the soul," she promises.

Chapter 20

our daily bread

They ambled into Venice from over by Culver City, pootling along – as they did with cheerful purpose – up and down the streets in all parts of L.A. and into the towns all around it: boxy blue and yellow emblems of an era, trawling the residential byways, selling fresh bread.

Heralded by its distinctive toot-toot, the Helms Bakery truck trundled forth upon the avenues of the Venetian neighborhoods, alert to the cardboard signs with the big blue letter "H" that housewives of the 1950s placed in their windows to signal a desire for a delivery of bakery goods. Inside the truck was organized with the sublime efficiency of a ship's galley. Passels of drawers rolled open to reveal cookies and cupcakes, donuts and Danish, breads and pies, all lined up neat as a row of lipsticks at the May Company.

Turned out with proud precision, the Helmsmen presented as a friendly platoon of the vaguely military, with the impressive addition to their uniforms of a cha-chinging metal change maker worn at their waists. Most were patient and funny and knew all of the kids on their route by name, enjoying the grimy gang of youngsters who swarmed them with the same eager enthusiasm they would bestow upon the Good Humor ice cream man. The Helmsman often gifted the children with tasty samples and sometimes even allowed them to *personally* deposit the coins for their purchases into his shiny silver change maker.

It all began in 1931, a relatively small venture, started by Paul Helms, Sr. with thirty-four employees and eleven sales routes. Within months Helms was not just concerned with emptying his heart into his infant operation, he was embroiled in the creation of a miracle.

Though a belated member of a throng of L.A. promoters and boosters, with breathtaking optimism Helms plunged in to do his bit towards saving from doom the 1932 Summer Olympic Games – set to be held in Los Angeles – against the overwhelming odds of a world as sunken in economic depression as the mastodons in the La Brea Tar Pits. That they pulled it off is, to this day, a source of admiration and amazement. His participation in the marvel earned Helms the designation of "The Official Olympics Games Bakers," and bestowed on his business the same kind of bold visibility associated with pink frosting flowers on a birthday cake.

The bakery initiative swelled like a loaf of bread on an overdose of yeast, exploding into a fleet of 500 trucks operating from a huge, specially built Zig-Zag Moderne structure out on Venice Boulevard in L.A. In 1936 his passion for sports led Helms to establish a nearby museum and library dedicated to athletics.

By the time the baby boomer generation came along, the Helms Bakery was supporting its community in more subtle ways too, putting multitudes of pint-sized scholars wise to the ways of commercial bread production. For kids in the Los Angeles City School District, it was part of a third grade multi-disciplinary social studies unit, beginning with research on farming, punctuated with off-key singing about amber waves of grain. Following this, they boarded a big yellow school bus for a thrilling field trip to the Helms Bakery, on a mission of discovery regarding the fate of those amber waves.

At the end of their visit, while still agog over the sight of the huge equipment and awe inspiring quantities of ingredients, Venice students received souvenirs consisting of a miniature loaf of bread and a small cardboard fold-together Helms truck, the acquisition of which could require months of serious eBay monitoring these days. The study culminated back in their classrooms with a review of what had been learned and perhaps, if their teacher was excessively courageous, topped off by their very own bread-making pageant – rehearsed with the soulful seriousness of a Shakespearean production – to which their moms might be invited to bear witness from a perch upon tiny, incommodious student chairs.

Surrendering to changing realities, in 1969 after its splendaciously elegant swan song sending bread to the moon via Apollo 11, the iconic enterprise toot-tooted its last. The Helms building, once a state-of-the-art bastion of bread making, now houses furniture stores, restaurants, a jazz venue and a charming little museum honoring its doughy genesis; while those quirky little blue and yellow trucks still loom fondly in the memories of all who once knew them.

the beat of a bongo the howl of a poet

It was a movement. Like Cubism. And like Cubism it was about experimentation and expression and was scorned – perhaps even feared – because its practitioners had slipped scandalously free of the inhibiting bondage of the conventional worldview. The principles of the Beat movement consisted of these: hanging out and heavy thinking and communicating – in whatever chosen mode – free loving, freeloading, under the influence of this substance or that.

The first and preeminent protagonists of the male centered Beat Generation – Allen Ginsberg, Jack Kerouac and William S. Burroughs – railed and incited. While art and jazz played syncopated counterpoint, the poets and writers were the Generation's true bling. Resplendent in beards and berets and black turtlenecks they peppered their speech with cool hepcat jargon and reeked of impassioned rebelliousness.

The main strongholds of Beatdom were New York's Greenwich Village and San Francisco's North Beach, but it was practically ordained that an outpost would take root in Venice. Disparaged as a "slum by the sea" they were attracted by its cheap rents and relative indifference to their ragtag way of life. If the surfers of Venice were born of the sun, the era-paralleling Beats were its children of the night.

The Venice Beats were not the Ivy League educated sons of bluebook families the New York Beats were. They had come to Venice, not to be part of a movement, but to dodge the whole responsibility-respectability-work thingy in favor of unfettered freedom as society dropouts. Relieved of the tyranny of material comfort, they were able to surrender to the sway of their own tangled thoughts as consigned to paper or canvas or the air. Some flew high above the flock, in giftedness, in craftsmanship: Stuart Perkoff, for example, who strove to create "visions for the tribe;" Charlie Foster, a once golden ad guy gone feral; and Alexander Trocchi, whose writing and very life were sacred offerings to the heroin god.

Then there was Larry Lipton, a 50-something whodunit co-author, literary novelist, journalist, screen and radio scriptwriter and poet. He applauded voluntary poverty for its holiness, advocated poetry as performance art, and he aspired to Big Bwana-ship of his own little cell of creative bohemians. He thus initiated Sunday afternoon gatherings of the shabby Venice disaffili-ates at his bungalow home, to school, mentor, encourage, rally, direct and serve sandwiches – a not unimportant consideration. Pretentiously, he dubbed these assemblies "Venice West."

Somewhat prematurely, Stuart Perkoff opened a coffeehouse – a Beat's natural habitat – at #7 Dudley. It, too, was called Venice West but it was more a salon than the guru's temple of the original. Purposefully grubby, it provided a venue for Venice art, poetry and jazz, a hipster rendezvous spot for Beat buddies. When Perkoff bailed out, first John Kenevan then finally John and Anna Haag became the proprietors of the dusk to dawn enclave of cool.

There were hordes of pretenders to the Beatster lifestyle who actually had jobs or were going to school. My friend Marilyn Slater remembers it almost as a summer romance. Correctly togged out in a black Mao jacket, she and her friends soaked up the scene's atmospheric vibes and earnestly debated political theologies between poets of often iffy aptitude howling epic elegies of death, punctuated by the beat of a bongo.

By this time Larry Lipton's new book, named for and exploi-tive of his "Holy Barbarians," had been published and he took a hand in the opening of a beatniks' private club cum flophouse cum Theatre of the Venice Beat: The Gas House at Market and Ocean Front Walk. Due to the crass notoriety these inflamed, crowds of the curious arrived – literally by busloads – to check out the Beats as if they were a clan of Abominable Snowmen in pink feather boas. The police weren't far behind, acting – to put it gently –as a hassle and botheration and firm disincentive to stick around.

The Beats of Venice were a group of disenchantees unwilling to take up middle class ways. They weren't, in the main, fame-seekers. Larry Lipton imposed that upon them, just as he had imposed their Beathood. What they wanted was to write, create art and make music – at whatever level of excellence – unnoticed and unencumbered by society's rules. Infamy got in the way.

Chapter 22

a philomene rhapsody

They are already ghosts
John and Philomene
As they pass
Along the Boardwalk
Where ghosts and poets overlap...
Philomene Long

More than two years after her passing, the silence of her absence from the streets and the sand of her cherished Venice milieu, still echoes like a great mournful wail. Left in the vacuum created by the loss of her, even the pigeons remain grieved, I fancy.

"She lived in the rapture of ideas," wrote the poet John O'Kane, a practice that began early; for by the age of eight Philomene Long was already drawn to the cloister, captured by the drama, the trappings, the whole mystical gestalt of it. She slipped into a nun's habit within the order of St. Joseph's of Carondelet in Los Angeles, immediately following her stint as a high school wild child. Five years later, she would jump the convent wall to be spirited off – in the dark of night – in a get-away car driven by her sister Pegarty.

Leaving the convent did not represent an abandonment of spirituality, or even a rejection of Catholicism. Instead, under the tutoring of Maezumi Roshi she would surrender to an immersion in Zen Buddhism that blended into a customized theology and to self-identification as a Zen-Catholic. Her poetry, too, became like an element of her faith walk.

It was poetry that brought her to Venice in 1968, pulled by its reputation for harboring the poor and poetic, but too late for the

Beat Generation's halcyon days. Still, she stayed and she carried on its traditions.

Poetry became her, in the way a fiery sunset is becoming to the western sky. Her range was boundless and included dreamy odes to the California Missions, a disturbingly vivid testimony regarding self-flagellation, a hilarious retelling of the winning homerun in a vintage baseball game, a little whine about leaky ceilings. She wrote poems in praise of a politician, in praise of Venice itself as "holy ground stained by the blood of poets," a fragment of the latter carved into Venice's Poetry Wall at Windward Plaza.

At readings she unleashed her words in a raspy, ravenesque voice wrapped in a dramatic cadence with just a wee Irish lilt on occasion: indeed, the ideal instrument for a howl of wrath or a purring caress and wielding the frank authority to proclaim the end of the world, should the situation arise. A master cobbler of poetic thought forms, Philomene was officially the Poet Laureate of Venice, so designated in an impressive commendation extolling her mind-enchanting, heart-inspiring, soul-uplifting talent and eloquence.

She was zany and mercurial. She was earthy and otherworldly. She was accustomed to the visibility that charisma endows, had been since the years of her youth.

A girl guru, gifted teacher, good friend; Philomene Long was all of these. At UCLA's extension school, she was a popular faculty member in the writing program, inciting her students to passion for the pleasures of poetry and fervor for its well-crafted creation. She was an ardent promoter of the Beyond Baroque literary center where she facilitated workshops and was an unfaltering supporter of its director Fred Dewey. She romped through her sister's film, *The Irish Vampire Goes West,* an eerie, fairy festooned tale about a poet snatched by a vampire and her sister's dogged rescue efforts.

He wasn't her first lover, nor even her first husband but the others were eclipsed by the coming – in 1983 – of the poet John Thomas, whom Philomene referred to as "my only one." Her twinship with Pegarty – of the monozygotic sort – was training for the concentrated relationship with Thomas, in which their two souls seemingly swirled into one.

Simmering in their commitment to one another and to their artistic exertions, they lived at the Ellison Apartments on Paloma Avenue. Although brazenly funky, it's a venerable brick structure built in 1914 with a sea view and a nesting place for pigeons outside the kitchen window and a creaky green iron gate one door up from the boardwalk. From here they embraced voluntary poverty and sallied forth into the bohemian enclave: the high priestess of the realm, and her beloved consort.

But always, Pegarty – her twin sister, twin star – was there as the wind beneath her wings. Now Philomene comes to her in recurring dreams, their monozygotic bond undiminished.

Chapter 23

wave riders

*He is driven by cresting swells of sound
toward the exotic shores of Scheherazade.*
Bill Gould

These days Bill Gould lives in South Dakota and drives a long train hauling coal. Whenever he can, he returns to the beaches of Southern California, a soul surfer returning to the sea.

He began, as a lad, watching older guys surf at the point where La Ballona Creek meets the Pacific at the south side of Venice. Three years later, when he was 14, his paper route funded the purchase of his first board, a 9^{ft}10^{in} Jacobs, upon which he was soon gliding across the swirling salty water along the beach at the north end of Venice, where the deserted Pacific Ocean Park still stood. Here the pier stuck out from the shore causing sand bars, advantageously making the waves break further out.

At age 11, Chipp Miller began surfing at the north end of Venice beach. He was there during the 1950s and '60s – the halcyon age of surfing – all shaggy blond hair and baggy pants and a generous blob of zinc oxide on his nose. He has memories of long boards, knee padding, trying to stay dry to stay warm. More memories of "morning fog enshrouding the end of the pier with waves rising out of the mist, smooth and glassy." He remembers school days cut short after receiving clandestine notes bearing the words: surf's up. "There have been few thrills in life to compare with the exhilaration brought on by those words," he told me.

The very first Venice surfer was here in 1907, a Hawaiian Islander named George Freeth, using the 200-pound, eight-foot-long wooden board of this own design. Described by adventure writer Jack London as "a young god bronzed with sunburn," Freeth was lugged to California by SoCal transportation and real estate tycoon Henry Huntington, who employed Freeth's surfing exhibitions as a lure to potential buyers to check out his new development at Redondo Beach.

In the mid-decades of the 20th century the surfing culture was fraught with idiosyncratic customs and accoutrements. There was a fondness for wood paneled station wagons – called Woodies – for St. Christopher medals or Tiki pendants, for cutoff Levi's, Van's canvas deck shoes, Mexican ponchos and – in the '60s – garb bearing labels such as Hang Ten or Birdwell Beach Britches. It had its own language too – slanguage, if you will – incorporating terms such as "shooting the curl" and "hodad" to define concepts unique to the surfers' way.

Beginning around 1960, the musical soundtrack of the surfing realm balanced Polynesian kitsch – awash in screaming monkeys and wailing macaws – with ripping and rumbling guitar riffs from the likes of Link Wray and Dick Dale. Of course, the unrivaled troubadours of the surfing life were the Beach Boys: they of the smooth vocal harmonies, the complex arrangements and spot-on evocations.

Trappings and trimmings aside, it's an intensely in-the-moment kind of pursuit. Both Miller and Gould – Freeth too, for all I know – are exponents of the transcendental school of surfing, as it were; called by its mysticism, its primeval connectivity, the mood changes of the sea. When they speak of it, there are soft echoes of Zen poets.

Fabulously photogenic, as early as the 1930s indie films were made venerating the lifeways of the surfer. They were intended for consumption in relatively small venues by surfing practitioners themselves.

A different sort of surf movie was released by Columbia Pictures in 1959. The true story of a congregation of Malibu wave bums who adopted as a kind of mascot a 16-year old girl with surfing aspirations, *Gidget* changed everything! Straight off there was a stampede of surfer posers crowding the beaches, igniting the surfer version of range wars.

Bound up as it was with the sea, the sand and the sun, no other lifestyle – not the dashing dons and beautiful senoritas of the sprawling Spanish land grant ranchos, not even the glitterescent Hollywood movie stars of the 1930s and '40s – defined the golden myth of Southern California as emblematically as the surfers of half a century ago did.

Venice never possessed the deluxe wave rider cachet of Malibu or La Jolla's Windansea. Some called it a beach ghetto, others said it was funky and it wasn't the best surfing beach at all. But the scene-sharing beatniks added a throbbing bohemianism to the Venice surfer gestalt.

Chipp Miller and Bill Gould were there. Sometimes.

Chapter 24

snake charmer

He was a tall, handsome stud-muffin of a dude, an archetypal Texan with dark curly hair, an amiable swagger and a work-a-day fast-car building uniform that consisted of boots, overalls and a big black Stetson hat.

Carroll Shelby had been a skinny, sickly kid whose heart condition later on would end his career as a boffo auto racer, but in 1962, standing in his brand new Cobra manufacturing plant in Venice, California, you sure wouldn't know it to look at him.

His love affair with racecars began almost simultaneously with the dawn of stock car and sprint car racing. He was just a little kid when his dad started taking him to the small, oval, dirt tracks – dubbed Bull Rings –– where, as Shelby described it, the "cars skidded on loose dirt, trying to claw their way round the turns under full throttle."

He was 29-years old, in 1952, when he climbed behind the wheel of a home-built MG-TC, outfitted with a flathead Ford engine, to drive in – and win – his first race at a quarter-mile drag strip. A few months later, he was back in his friend Ed's MG again, roaring around a triangular course – each lap a mile or a mile and a half – against a passel of other MGs in the first race, then driving the only MG against a bunch of Jaguar XK120s for the second, finally driving an XK120, himself, against other XK120 Jags.

He skunked them all that day.

For several months, he caught recurring rides in burly, British Allard sports cars powered by pumped-up Cadillac engines. It was at this time that the striped farm overalls made their debut as Shelby's signature togs, in contrast to the other racers' much snappier duds.

Pretty soon he was making good on the European circuit, "the cradle of motor racing:" winning friends with his irresistible, throwaway charm that pushed him to the top of the popularity heap; winning races, too, driving Aston Martins, Ferraris, Maseratis, Porsches and suchlike.

More than once he was damaged in significant crashes.

He was twice named *Sports Illustrated*'s Driver of the Year. With co-driver Ray Salvadori he won the 24 Hours of Le Mans. One year he was the Sports Car Club of America's driving champion. But during the 1960 season, though thundering forward at breathtaking speeds as usual, Carroll Shelby often had a nitroglycerine tablet tucked firmly beneath his tongue to ease the chronic pain in his chest.

Fortunately, as an apparent inheritor of the acrobatically adaptive Abbot Kinney dream-chaser gene, he knew when to yield to what's so and revise his ambition to suit the situation. While the "yen to drive racecars," was for Shelby, "a thing that burns like a bright, unquenchable flame which nothing can put out;" he realized that he needed to flush that notion as the empowering belief of his life. Dusting himself off, he simply changed his position within the racing paradigm.

By then he was hot to be *building* cars anyway.

The force was surely with him, allowing Shelby to wire up a sublime synthesis of an original English A.C. sports car chassis and body with a 260-cubic inch Ford engine. And do it with no upfront cash.

He took up occupancy in March of 1962 at Lance Reventlow's old Scarab racecar factory on Princeton Drive in Venice, next to Owen Keon Chevrolet. Here adjustment and amendment and alteration went on relentlessly. Here assembly could rattle forth on five vehicles at a time: mean street machines and competition cars too.

The roadsters clocked their first win just ten months later. The very next year they would win the United States Road Racing Championship. A few months after that, the engine muscle was majorly beefed up with a hefty Ford 427.

It came in a dream, the reptilian name for Shelby's spectacular new sports car, and was promptly glommed, one assumes, for the psychological fear factor a snake inspires. An actual *live* Cobra, in its own glass habitat moved into the shop to assume the job of official mascot. The serpent was the cause of great consternation when it somehow escaped from its confines to go missing for several days, and was summarily fired upon its recapture.

Carroll Shelby abided in Venice only briefly, just long enough to bring his business from a startup of nothing to a $16 million dollar company in 1965. Then the need for greater production space dictated he swagger on.

Chapter 25

the devotee's labyrinth

Pat Hartman is a compulsive devotee of Venice, California. She reads about it, writes about it, paints it and serves as hand-maiden-in-charge of an online shrine for its veneration. Actually, she defines herself as the "webslave." "Virtualvenice.info" is like an intricate little labyrinth, all twists and turns crammed full of Venice facts, fancies and lists. The unwary visitor might find herself lost in it for days. It's best to take a sandwich along.

Hartman arrived in Venice in 1978, called to it like a lemming, unaware that it would consume her with the inevitability of the cliffs lemmings are notorious for overrunning. She settled right into the area called Oakwood, which at the time was distinguished by its status as L.A.'s #2 crime scene. She and her 11-year old biracial daughter moved in with a roomie (and her daughter) met through an ad in a publication called *The Recycler*. To the left of them were WASPs with a fine vegetable garden, to the right a multi-unit hive of recent border crossers playing loud Mexican music, across the street were quiet Chinese living next door to a large and rowdy black family, behind was an alley, above an actor and a musician. Radical diversity was a big part of the neighborhood's appeal.

She lived in Venice for six years, chronicling her term here in detailed diaries that, upon attaining distance in geography and epoch, Hartman would translate into writings for general consumption. In language possessed of an amiable, jaunty swagger she tells of her strangely mystical sojourn in books that are something like an ant farm fostering a view of the life of its inhabitants inside. Hartman divided her "farm" into two parts: the public life and the private.

Sassy and saucy, her account of the private, *Ghost Town: A Venice, California Life,* is like a would-be model for a sad, hilarious, multihued television sit-com just lolling around waiting for a producer with the prescience, guts and integrity to take it up.

Call Someplace Paradise opens with the statement, "Venice is a Los Angeles coastal community like sex is a biological function." It hurtles forward from there to document the fervor-fomenting politics, the seething arts scene, the community's at-once congenial and combative character, as they existed twenty-five or thirty years ago. Pat Hartman's passion and presence and participation suggest a level of energy generated by a nuclear power plant and a brain that's the size of Minnesota.

She's also written a raft of unpublished short stories set in the Venice milieu. One of them, "Bent Out of Shape" can be seen and read on her website.

Pootling about Hartman's Virtual Venice is like eating an artichoke: each leaf a separate indulgence. Behind the colorful little flags acting as doorsills to the site's variety and vagaries lie variations on the theme of her philosophy that "Venice, like the sun, is both gravity and radiance."

The website has a bulletin board upon which Venice residents – past and present – thumbtack word snapshots of their tenure here, most of them tinged with grateful nostalgia for a halcyon era of freedom. Then there's a lengthy catalog of books, in which Venice figures, and a similar inventory of movies. There are to be found old postcard images, a collection of Venice quotations, archives of the *Free Venice Beachhead*. Here are sections given over to the poetry and to the music and to the visual artists of Venice. There are other sections on Hartman's own books and her paintings and a "virtual boardwalk" where stuff is for sale. The whole of it throbs with the eccentric liveliness of Ocean Front Walk itself.

Earthy and arty, Pat Hartman was drawn to the arty weirdness of Venice and during her stay here she invested her heart and soul in it; but then it was time to move on. She had learned that for her "Venice is a state of mind" and that it was therefore portable. Besides, her volunteer web slavery keeps her connection alive.

"Who can explain the allure and mystique of Venice Beach as a place of legend, a New World Shangri-La?" she asks. Hartman, herself, does a pretty good job of it.

Here is the link to her Internet labyrinth: http://www.virtual-venice.info

Chapter 26

now appearing

I want to be complex. I want to be simple. I want to be the naked, glistening stranger. We all want to be special.
                                                            Peter Demian

It's not a cushy life. At 62 he still makes the rent by huffing and puffing, moving and hauling. But evenings and on weekends he's to be found down on Ocean Front Walk making his music, living his dream.

Peter Demian first pootled into Venice, California in 1978, at the suggestion of the policeman who busted him for camping out in his car on Mulholland Drive. Relocating the 1969 Valiant to the Rose Lane Parking lot, he stayed on to become a gravelly-voiced fixture of the freewheeling, ragamuffin milieu.

Thirty years later he practically qualifies as a historic figure as well as a continuing contributor to the town's signature element: that gaggle of full-blown eccentrics made up in part by a chainsaw juggler, a fire-eater, a nearly naked guy standing atop a ladder playing with snakes, a turbaned guitar player on rollerblades, a gold spray-painted mime and a raft of fortune tellers as well as the whole host of music makers and artists of all stripes. In fact, an oddball facsimile of what Abbot Kinney had in mind when he started the place. More or less.

For a couple of decades he staked out Bench #5, across from Figtree's restaurant, as his own personal venue. Several months ago he was shifted to a spot across from The Side Walk Café, due to his new amplification. It's an auspicious location as it allows the meal-eating public ample time to hear and appreciate the music, resulting in more generous tips. Away from such audience-detainers, the crowds are "like clouds going by," Peter says, only occasionally stopping to drop a monetary acknowledgement into the open guitar case.

Like the gypsy musical form of flamenco, Peter's music is throaty and raw and impassioned. He sings about the bag ladies, palm trees and the cold winter breezes that texture his world – amalgamating the mundane and the profound with insouciant flourish – creating gritty odes on the life of a rock n' roll poet that spring from the depths of his soul. His CD, *Paloma Serenade,* captures and holds eleven of his tuneful dabs of poetry, like grainy black-and-white photos nailed to a wall.

Hang out with Peter Demian for a while and you're likely to hear some of his stories. For instance, one time he was so broke he sold his television set, then his radio. The sound of the silence was so deafening he turned on the vacuum cleaner for something to listen to. It's a sweet story of adaptability – and attitude – that brings forth smiles and chuckles: the *real* point of the tale. "Without humor you fall over," he offers, in one of his fortune-cookie-sized bits of wisdom.

Peter was the focus of a chapter in book called *Passing the Hat: Street Performers in America* by Patricia J. Campbell; and in a segment of *Loose Change,* an Emmy Award winning documentary, produced and directed by Phil Reeder, who was "wonderfully impressed by both Peter's talent as a performer and by his personal charisma." Their attention didn't turn him into a household name but the spotlighting chronicles – of this sidewalk philosopher – gave him even broader exposure than he's already accustomed to with the multi-thousands of people who amble along Venice's bohemian boardwalk on any pleasant Sunday afternoon.

Peter Demian likes people. He treats his audience like cherished friends; other musicians drop by to jam. A lone skater may choreograph a spontaneous dance, while others twirl about in their own little boogies. As the sun slowly slinks into the sea, Peter bids it adieu with the "Sunset Song," its innumerable verses ever changing, ever modifying to incorporate some of those who are present.

The lifestyle ain't easy. But it's far from impoverished. He has the love of a good woman and their 18 year-old son.

"I'm not famous or rich," he says, "but I'm doing what I love. At 62, I'm still playing my music and I still have my hair."

Chapter 27

a dog, a bunny, an ad guy

What is advertising...the most exciting, the most arduous literary form of all, the most difficult to master, the most pregnant in curious possibilities.
Aldous Huxley

In the realm of advertising Lee Clow is legendary. An intrepid interpreter of who we are as a society, he is also the pop culture architect who brought forth such icons as the Energizer Bunny and the Taco Bell Chihuahua; the creative director cum motivational marketeer who spawned Nike's "Never Give Up" and Apple's "Think Different" ads. For many years the brilliant effects of his persuasive genius emanated from the right here in Venice, a place with which he shares some defining qualities: like casualness, quirkiness and iconoclasm.

His scaling of the heights of ad guy greatness began with the recognition of his artistic talent by his first grade teacher, Mrs. Rice, followed by his mother's cheerleading for the development of said talent. He went to art school after high school, was drafted during the Vietnam War, which he spent at the White Sands Missile Range in New Mexico. His military obligation fulfilled, he went to art school some more. Hired by a Los Angeles ad shop, he was appalled by the mediocrity of its work.

Clow admired what DDB was doing, but nixed New York; he did *not* want to wear a suit nor did he want his career to interfere with his surfing. So he studied up on what his native SoCal had to offer, identified Chiat-Day as his employer of choice and promptly undertook a saturation campaign on Jay Chiat. In 1971 he nailed that position he wanted so badly. His convictions, his blossoming skill-set, his passion were in perfect sync with Chiat-Day, where the shorts and T-shirts and flip-flops representing his personal style of business fashion became just another aspect of his mythology.

Lee Clow doesn't like the label "advertising" for what he does now, he prefers the term "media art." While there may be a whiff of the highfalutin to his preferred terminology, there is no denying that he has often carried communication to a lofty art form. "You know all those posters Toulouse-Lautrec did? Those were ads," he reminds, making his point.

The truth is, due to changes in the biz wrought by changes in technology and media proliferation over the past decade or two, his craft has radically expanded from the billboards and magazine ads and the 30-second TV commercials of yesteryear, even beyond his own "1984," Mac computer-introducing Super Bowl ad, still considered the best commercial of all time and the beginning of advertising as an event in its own right.

These days the mission of this promotional maven is more holistic. It includes all of the above in addition to harnessing the Internet plus such "branding" enterprises as designing customer-immersing retail stores for Apple or engineering new bottles for Gatorade. He acted as life coach in assisting Pepsi and Pedigree through a "personal growth" kind of process challenging themselves to be *more* than just manufacturers of soda pop or dog food but to be companies known, too, for highly developed senses of social consciousness.

In his book *Adcult*, James B. Twitchell promulgates the idea that advertising is the "dominant meaning-making system of modern life," a thought form with which Clow surely concurs.

He publishes a little Twitter blog called "Lee Clow's Beard." It's a collection of Zen-like dabs of insight, mostly on the subject of making ads, such as, "Just because it's measurable doesn't mean it matters," or "Ubiquity is a poor substitute for uniqueness." My personal favorite is more general in nature, "A mistake is just another way of doing things."

As his blog aptly demonstrates, Clow's gene pool – metaphorically speaking – contains more Plato than P.T. Barnum DNA. But while he might care how many iPods are sold, it is the prospect of creative luminosity in the work that is the soul of his motivation, what he strives to achieve. Not infrequently, this creativity-as-the-driving-force has caused conflicts between the agency and its clients, resulting in complaints of arrogance and failure to listen by the companies they "served" – and were ultimately fired by. It is said that Chiat-Day has lost more primo accounts than most agencies ever land.

This man *Advertising Age* dubbed "advertising's art director guru," no longer operates out of Venice, California, the TBWA/Chiat-Day offices moved southward near Playa Del Rey some years ago. Yet he still radiates that certain Venetian insouciance, its earthy, eccentric charisma.

in the vernacular

*Anything haywire is always most
haywire in Southern California.*
The Architectural Forum, 1935

Sometimes they call it vernacular architecture – or program-
matic, or figurative, or novelty or roadside or mimetic. By whatever name, it's kitsch in the first degree. And though California
was not actually its birthplace it became its most natural setting,
the 1920s and '30s the golden age of this eccentric architectural
form.

Radiating with goofy surrealism, the fanciful form was defined
in such oddball manifestations as florist shops in the shape of a
flowerpot, a hot dog stand housed in a large cement hot dog, or
an ice cream store supported by gigantic ice cream cone pillars.
Potentiated by the Southern California auto culture, they served
as high visibility advertising beacons for whatever the inspired
owner was selling, but the come-on was not always so symbolically concrete. The hamburger purveyor might opt, instead, for a
building contoured after a zeppelin or a toad rather than after a
hamburger. A bakery might do business out of a windmill.

Quirky small business owners enshrined their rinky-dink
operations in all manner of whimsical expressions shaped like
airplanes and teapots, pigs and pianos, hats and shoes. Most of
them are sadly long gone, flushed by a society that takes itself too
seriously to snarf lunch in a construction that looks like a pit bull.

Happily, one of the last examples of this lively architectural
genre resides right here in Venice at 340 Main Street, south of
Rose Avenue. The four-story Binocular Building, was designed

in 1985 by Frank Gehry as the home of the hot ticket Chiat-Day advertising agency, but was not completed till 1991 due to a little toxicity issue. Today it stands there, incomparable in presentation and true in spirit to its peculiar vernacular roots.

Venice figured prominently on Frank Gehry's pathway towards international esteem for his occupancy accommodating sculptures with huge zowie factors. In 1962, after a year lolling around Paris marinating in the work of modernist pioneer Le Corbusier, Gehry returned to the U.S. and opened a studio in Santa Monica. But it was in nearby funked-out, Beat-Generation-sheltering Venice that he found his true kindred spirits. Here he hooked up with a little assembly of freethinking artists – 16 of them to be exact – from whom he received the stimulation and encouragement to go off in a whole new direction with his work, creating unconventional buildings with a kinship to collages fashioned from found materials.

As time passed the architectural savant would go on to evolve further embracing a "deconstructed aesthetic," in which he would "explode familiar geometric volumes and reassemble them in original new forms of unprecedented complexity," according to his Academy of Achievement biography.

Certainly Gehry's celebrated Binocular Building meets the definition of complex – if for no other reason than its fearless disregard of cohesiveness – being, really, a rather weird set of mismatched triplets lined up one beside the other but evincing no noticeable relationship. To the left reclines a vaguely ship-like, gentle curve of white with hyphenesque windows streaking along the sidewalk-facing wall; to the right a dark, looming configuration, a giant rusty iron doorstop of a thing posed like a bullfrog with its back to the street.

Situated between these two, providing a gateway to the three-level parking garage below and housing twin conference rooms above, is the life-like namesake binocular sculpture created by Gehry's artist friends-and-collaborators, Claes Oldenburg and his wife Coosje van Bruggen.

Jay Chiat was as far outside the box, thought wise, as Frank Gehry himself and what he ordered up was a "clubhouse" for creatives devoid of any whiff of the ordinary white-collar work-place, both inside and out.

After Chiat/Day bestirred themselves into new quarters, another bigwig ad agency, DDB Worldwide, took possession for several years. In January 2011 Google signed a lease to make the Binocular Building their own 75,000 square foot Southern California citadel, an especially congruent marriage of metaphors it seems to me – both Google and binoculars about bringing clarity as they are – inaugurating a modern instance of the symbolically concrete vernacular.

painting the town

Street murals are important to urban living – they focus on a city's culture, both past and present. Rip Cronk's murals add incredible beauty and depth to the landscape.
Patricia Nolan Stein

It is more than thirty years ago now that he breezed into town with public art on his mind. Already Rip Cronk had earned a reputation as a muralist of consequence for his work on public wallspace in Honolulu. His arrival in Venice clearly had *destiny* tattooed all over it, for almost immediately he came across a mural-painter-seeking ad placed by SPARC, the Social and Public Art Resource Center, an organization with which he promptly aligned and still maintains a solid association.

The mural form boasts a long lineage sweeping back all the way to 30,000 BC and the Chauvet Cave in what is now Southern France. Barreling forward historically, they appeared in ancient Egyptian tombs and Minoan palaces. They were practically ubiquitous during the Renaissance and were an evangelizing medium for Mexican *muralistas'* political statements in the 1930s.

Murals, of course, are a distinguishing component of Venice, California's kinky savoir-faire. It's oldest, *Kinney's Dream* painted by Edward Biberman in 1941, is to be found inside the post office. But the trend for Venice murals really kicked off in 1969 with *Brooks Street Painting*, a long gone collaboration between artists Terry Schoonhoven and Victor Henderson.

Cronk's first mural, painted in 1980 in this place he considers to be a cultural vortex, was *Venice on the Halfshell* that beckoned from the old Venice Pavilion, until it was summarily demolished.

Venice Reconstituted was it's spiritual replacement that went up in 1989 at Speedway and Windward. Newly morphed into *Venice Kinesis*, like its predecessors, it's a tasty variation on a theme of Botticelli's Birth of *Venus*, featuring a long-legged blonde beauty and a sprinkling of well-know Venetian personalities.

He has painted towering images of Abbot Kinney and Jim Morrison, a salute to Van Gogh's *Starry Night*, gatherings of slumming old time celebrities, a gondola ferrying a little covey of costumed high school students. He's painted a view of himself, dangling high up on a building spray-painting "Venice" across a blue sky. He's painted white-capped waves and a fanciful chorus line of cheerfully mismatched critters symbolizing a congenial multiethnic fraternity. And more.

His murals are accessible, humorous, iconic.

Subject to the effects of the sun and the wind, the salty air and unruly taggers, to remain vivid the murals require ongoing upkeep. As he works, whether on rehabs or new visions, Cronk enjoys being a part of – and an observer of – the life flow of Venice as it whirls about like eddying tide pools. "The boardwalk is a cultural event that happens everyday," he states. It brings him new inspiration and incipient conceptions that find their way into his notebooks bursting with ideas for future projects. It is the location, he says – or sometimes the location's wannabe culture-bestowing owner – that determines which possibilities will blossom.

Rip Cronk is a man with a mission wrapped up inside painting the town. It's about democratizing art, putting it out there for the poor and unwashed and everyone else, rather than addressing it exclusively to the gallery-going elite.

"The community mural de-alienates and delineates the individual in society," he opines, providing a subliminal invitation to communal connectivity. He does, however, subscribe to the notion which holds that the meaning of art resides as much in the viewer's perception as it does in the artist's intent.

Cronk believes artists – and other cultural creatives – have an obligation to provide emblems of the changing 21st century social order and also to resist the tendency towards despiritualization. He shares the 1914 viewpoint of English art critic Clive Bell that the merit of art lies in the expression of the "vital force" and the emotive bond the artist builds with the viewer through his work.

Cogitating on these things, he wrote a series of erudite essays that can be found at: www.rcronk.com. In them he considers the end of the modernist era in art and society and the dawning of a new cultural paradigm.

Processing it all into a personal creed, Cronk gives us joyful murals, which uniquely define the culture of this idiosyncratic townspot they adorn.

"It's always a treat to see his murals whenever I'm driving down the street or walking near the ocean, says journalist Patricia Nolan Stein. "I love Rip Cronk."

Chapter 30

shtick, tics
& klutzy savoir-faire

They've been making movies here for over a hundred years; the filmed visage of Venice plainly visible to the masses – during its golden periods and its funky – in motion pictures beginning with Mary Pickford's 1910 short, *Never Again*. They include a passel of "Our Gang" comedies, *A Touch of Evil* and *Arachnophobia*, *Grease* and *Get Shorty*, a whole raft of Roger Corman flicks. And *Fletch*.

Originating in Gregory Mcdonald's 1974 book of the same name, Fletch is investigative reporter Irwin Fletcher. He's in undercover mode, hot on the trail of a story that, beneath his "Jane Doe" byline – "What the hey, it's better than Irwin" – will expose the major source behind drug trafficking on the beach.

Simultaneously, a Jaguar-driving, upscale executive type has noticed him lolling about on the sand – vagrant junky style – and wants to pay Fletch big bucks to kill him. Now what's up with *that*?

Also known for his screenplays on cinema daff-fests like *Blazing Saddles, Soapdish* and *The In-Laws*, Andrew Bergman re-modeled Mcdonald's book into a customized vehicle for its zany star. Bergman banished the noir tone of the novel – praised upon publication as "the toughest, meanest horse to hit the literary racetrack since James M. Cain" – embracing instead a more loosey-goosey quality for the movie, reveling in its flood of low-budget disguises and the misappropriated names of Igor Stravinsky, Harry S. Truman, Gordon Liddy, Don Corleone.

Playing Irwin Fletcher, Chevy Chase is quite alluring, if you happen to like tall, handsome smart alecks with a cleft of Grand Canyon proportions in their chin. With obvious glee he flings himself into the occupation of one loopy persona after another, clearly enjoying his ersatz multiple personality disorder and bringing to bear the kind of wild-witted communication unseen since Groucho Marx was so adroitly manipulating the language.

The dialog Andrew Bergman wrote for the film, wedded to Chase's own wacky ad-libs, makes for a banquet of belly laughs. In its day, *Fletch* was the epitome of pop culture cool – a cult film even – and the nitzie guffaw-getters provided a rich vein of self-amusing pleasures to be mined by the legion of *Fletch* fanboys as they pitched bits of dialog and their one-liner responses back and forth to one another like Frisbees.

Chevy Chase is a wizard of brilliant improvisation and dead-pan delivery. *Fletch* is *his* movie – his best – and he acquits himself in it with magnificent, demented distinction. But he receives plenty of able support.

There's Tim Matheson, as executive guy Alan Stanwyk, who is – evidently – looking to engineer his own murder; Dana Wheeler-Nicholson is on tap as Gail Stanwyk, his neglected, slightly bimboesque wife. Richard Libertini appears as Fletch's life endangering editor; Joe Don Baker sashays about oozing smarm and menace as the police chief. Here too is Kareem Abdul-Jabbar pulling a cameo while Geena Davis is absolutely darling, squeezing into a part much too small for her towering presence and talents.

And Venice? Seen in glimpses, playing itself most aptly defined by terms like "unsavory," "insalubrious" or "seedy," is integral to the screwball authenticity of the production. In 1984, when location filming was going on, Venice was still pretty slummy, don'cha know, with lots of super shady sketch stuff boldly going down.

Wrapped up in a standard 1980s synthesizer-soaked soundtrack, director Michael Ritchie keeps his movie's action racing along at an Indy-car-worthy velocity and though it holds up just swell as an entertaining thriller, *Fletch* is considered a film comedy classic. In it, Chevy Chase is at the acme of his astounda-monsity prowess. The re-imagined version of Mcdonald's Irwin

Fletcher character is a sublime showcase for his inimitable brand of shtick, tics and klutzy savoir-faire. The plot flies about in pleasing convolutions.

And Venice Beach makes the perfect sleazy stage.

Chapter 31

founding father

*He recognized the richness of Venice's history and
made it possible to be passed on to future generations.*
Betsy Goldman

This year is the Venice Historical Society's twenty-fifth anniversary. Long overdue in formation, in 1986 a wee crowd of the conservation-minded broke through the apathy to take up the task of preserving the history of this certifiably screwball community, officially a district of the amorphous City of Los Angeles but still as distinct as a duck in a family of chickens.

That the history-saving society materialized was due to the effort of Don Tollefson, who leapt into the void to assume the lead, in the way of a dynamic caped crusader. Having been a meeting-attending member of the Los Angeles Conservancy he was already familiar with how these things worked.

Venice, California was a "bedraggled area, where no one cared and no one wanted to visit," he recalls, but by the mid-1980s things were starting to turn around, aroused by young people whose interest in the funky enclave was coaxing the rents and property prices onto an upward trajectory. Tollefson was one of those "interested" young property purchasers.

He came from Salem, Oregon in 1968, a seeker after SoCal's incredibly wonderful weather. He settled for a spell into L.A.'s Westside before easing further west to Venice in 1979, where he felt like he'd discovered "the center of the universe."

Perceiving Venice as spiritually akin to New York's Greenwich Village or San Francisco's Haight-Ashbury, "It was clear to me," he says, "that if anyplace deserved a historical society, Venice did."

Tollefson began in May of 1986, by placing an announcement in the *Los Angeles Times,* requesting contact by anyone who wanted to help with the establishment of a Venice conservancy group. He and the folks who came forward each pitched in $100.00. The resulting $1000.00 bankrolled the incorporation of the incipient history keeping organization.

Smoldering with purpose and enthusiasm, they came together for the first time in September of 1986, the founding family – so to speak – made up of Joan Del Monte, Betsy Goldman, Helga Hanssen, George Lenny, Phil Parlett, Mary Jane Weil, Vivi Wiitala, a representative of the Venice-Marina Board of Realtors and, of course, Don Tollefson himself.

Remembering those times, his friend, the writer Joan Del Monte says "He had tremendous energy, and came on strong for preservation when the sculptor Robert Graham demolished one of the columns in front of his studio on Windward Avenue."

"He [Tollefson] was a tall, gorgeous body builder," she continues, "and although he was a lawyer he worked as a bouncer at a club on Main Street in Santa Monica," employment which seemed to add a certain suitable cachet to the résumé of the newly elected VHS president, a position he would hold for two two-year terms.

What he envisioned for his little foundling association was a group of Venice history-esteeming members, bi-monthly meetings, a newsletter and the collection of archives. It was a vision he ferried into fruition creating the DNA imparting gene pool of the modern VHS manifestation. "The 21st century format is not much changed from days of yore," he says, " since we started with a really good blueprint."

Don Tollefson gracefully declined a recent invitation to return to the Board of Directors. These days he considers his role to be that of frequent and reliable financial contributor to VHS special projects. President Jill Prestup provides periodic updates and he couldn't be more pleased with the things the Society is doing and accomplishing.

Take, for example, the colonnade restoration. "It's fantastic!" he exclaims. "VHS picked a fabulous project. The colonnades are the crown jewel of Venice historical architecture. Nowhere else in the U.S is there anything comparable. I'd like to see them get a National Preservation designation."

Despite the fact that he is no longer rippin' and runnin' about in pursuit of VHS objectives, Venice, California still figures prominently in Tollefson's current ruling passion, which is the refurbishment of vintage properties, to "leave this place a better place," he says, and to promote it as a vacation destination. His fashioning of vacation rentals involves the restoration of the exteriors while dolling up the interiors into sleek, up-scale, amenity-boasting bastions of comfort and beauty. One such delightsome property is a 1913 California Craftsman bungalow commonly known locally as "Charlie Chaplin's Old House," a designation lavishly free of any supporting documentation, as Tollefson is quick to point out.

As we celebrate the Venice Historical Society's silver anniversary we need to remember and thank Don Tollefson who brought the whole thing into being.

credits & kisses

...for the dishy cover illustration from a 1923 postcard, published by the Van Ornum Colorprint Company in Los Angeles.

...for the title of this book gleaned from a tourist brochure published by the Southern Pacific Railroad in 1920.

...for the charming little seahorse at the book's beginning created especially for *The Lure of a Land by the Sea* by my dear friend Marilyn Slater who also generously serves as editor, cheerleader, researcher and writing sister.

...for the other cherished writer-sisters of my personal support squad, talented prose crafters Virginia Clifford Anders and Laura Shepard Townsend.

...for English professor/mentor/flame fanner of writing passion, Conrad Bayley, who many years ago nurtured the skills needed to scurry past mere enthusiasm.

...for Team Fusion "The Fabulous" at CreateSpace, for taking my words and my vision and transmogrifying them into this book.

...and for the sponsor of this book's publication, my beloved George Hanney, whose relentless encouragement and support have sustained me in ever-so-many ways over the years.

also by delores hanney

Venice, California: A Centennial Commemorative in Postcards

Mabel in Paradise: A Southern California Journal in Vintage Postcards (a website pretending to be silent screen comedienne Mabel Normand's personal collection of 1912-1930 postcards, assembled within an album and annotated by the star) found at: http://www.mabel-in-paradise.webs.com/

about the author

Phoenix, Arizona may seem like a pretty odd place for a Venice, California historian to reside but it is from Phoenix that I sashay along, following my dream as it beckons, researching and writing about Los Angeles and vicinity – honed in most keenly on Venice. It is the muse that has crooned to me since shortly after I arrived there as a tiny toddler at the end of World War II. Its sweet song has, at all times, invited me to bask languorously in its past with absolute abandon, but my hunger for its history remains ever unsated.

Delores Hanney

Made in the USA
Charleston, SC
02 August 2012